CQ's POCKET GUIDE TO THE LANGUAGE OF CONGRESS

CQ's POCKET GUIDE TO THE LANGUAGE OF CONGRESS

Congressional Quarterly Inc.
Washington, D.C.

Cover design: Kachergis Book Design

Copyright © 1994 Congressional Quarterly Inc.
1414 22nd Street, N.W., Washington, D.C. 20037

All rights reserved. No part of this publication may be reproduced or transmitted in any form or by any means, electronic or mechanical, including photocopying, recording, or any information storage and retrieval system, without permission in writing from the publisher.

Printed in the United States of America

Library of Congress Cataloging-in-Publication Data

CQ's pocket guide to the language of Congress
    p.   cm.
  ISBN 0-87187-995-6
  1. United States.   Congress—Dictionaries.
2. Legislation—United States—Dictionaries.
3. United States—Politics and government—
Dictionaries.   I. Congressional Quarterly Inc.
JK9.C67   1994
328.73'003—dc20   94-726
                                                      CIP

Editor's Note

CQ's Pocket Guide to the Language of Congress is a handy source of definitions and brief explanations of many terms and expressions in current use in the U.S. Congress. Most of the entries focus on the legislative process and particularly on congressional procedures, but a few deal with other subjects, such as organization, staff, and officers of Congress. Wherever appropriate, the explanations point out differences in procedure, practice, and terminology between the House of Representatives and the Senate and, when such information is available, between the political parties in each house. Many of the terms are illustrated with examples from history or include the historical origins of the word.

Congressional Quarterly is indebted to Walter Kravitz, whose work on the *American Congressional Dictionary* forms the basis for this book. Walter Kravitz is a teacher, lecturer, and private consultant on congressional organization and procedures. Previously, Kravitz was the senior expert on Congress at the Congressional Research Service. During his twenty-two years at CRS, Kravitz assisted House and Senate committees in developing proposals on virtually every facet of congressional organization, operations, administration, rules and procedural systems. He assisted in the development of the Legislative Reorganization Act of 1970 and was the first executive director of the House Budget Committee.

Congressional Quarterly Inc., an editorial research service and publishing company, serves clients in the fields of news, education, business, and government. It combines the specific coverage of Congress, government, and politics contained in the *Congressional Quarterly Weekly Report* with the more general subject range of an affiliated service, the *CQ Researcher*.

Congressional Quarterly also publishes a variety of books, including college political science textbooks under the CQ Press imprint and public affairs paperbacks on developing issues and events. CQ Books researches, writes, and publishes information directories and reference books on the federal government, national elections, and politics, including the *Guide to the Presidency*, the *Guide to Congress*, the *Guide to the U.S. Supreme Court*, the *Guide to U.S. Elections*, and *Politics in America*. *CQ's Encyclopedia of American Government* is a three-volume reference work providing essential information about the U.S. government. The *CQ Almanac*, a compendium of legislation for one session of Congress, is published each year. *Congress and the Nation*, a record of government for a presidential term, is published every four years.

A

Absolute Majority A vote requiring approval by a majority of all members of a house rather than a majority of members present and voting.

Act A bill passed in identical form by both houses of Congress and signed into law by the president or enacted over his veto. A bill also becomes an act without the president's signature if he does not return it to Congress within ten days (Sundays excepted) and if Congress has not adjourned within that period.

Ad Hoc Select Committee A temporary committee formed for a special purpose or to deal with a specific subject.

Adjourn A formal motion to end a day's session or meeting of a house or a committee. A motion to adjourn usually has no conditions attached to it, but it may specify the day or time for reconvening or make reconvening subject to the call of the chamber's presiding officer or the committee's chairman. In both houses, a motion to adjourn is of the highest privilege, takes precedence over all other motions, is not debatable, and must be put to an immediate decision. Adjournment of a house ends its legislative day.

Adjourn for More Than Three Days Under Article I, Section 5 of the Constitution, neither house may adjourn for more than three days without the approval of the other. The necessary approval is given in a concurrent resolution and agreed to by both houses, which may permit one or both to take such an adjournment.

Adjournment by July 31 The Legislative Reorganization Act of 1946 requires Congress to adjourn sine die no later than July 31 of each year unless Congress provides otherwise. Except in 1952 and 1956, Congress has provided otherwise.

Adjournment Sine Die Final adjournment of an annual or two-year session of Congress; literally, adjournment without a day. The two houses must agree to a privileged concurrent resolution for such an adjournment. A sine die adjournment precludes Congress from meeting again until the next constitutionally fixed date of a session (January 3 of the following year) unless Congress determines otherwise by law or the president calls it into special session.

Article II, Section 3 of the Constitution authorizes the president to adjourn both houses until such time as he thinks proper when the two houses cannot agree to a time of adjournment, but no president has ever exercised this authority.

Adjournment to a Day (and Time) Certain An adjournment that fixes the next date and time of meeting for one or both houses. It does not end an annual session of Congress.

Administration Bill A bill drafted in the executive office of the president or in an executive department or agency to implement part of the president's program.

Administrative Assistant (AA) The title usually given to a member's chief aide, political advisor, and head of office staff.

Adoption The usual parliamentary term for approval of a conference report. It is also commonly applied to amendments.

Advance Appropriation In an appropriation act for a particular fiscal year, an appropriation that does not become available for spending or obligation until a subsequent fiscal year.

Adverse Report A committee report recommending against approval of a measure or some other matter. Committees usually pigeonhole measures they oppose instead of reporting them adversely, but they may be required to report them by a statutory rule or an instruction from their parent body.

Advice and Consent The Senate's constitutional role in consenting to or rejecting the president's nominations to executive branch and judicial offices and the treaties he submits. Confirmation of nominees requires a simple majority vote of the full Senate. Treaties must be approved by a two-thirds majority of senators present and voting.

Agency Generic term for a governmental organization, such as a department, bureau, office, commission, board, administration, advisory council, and so forth.

Agency Debt Federal debt incurred by an agency authorized to borrow money from the public or from other government funds or accounts.

Agreed to The usual parliamentary term for approval of motions, amendments, and simple and concurrent resolutions.

Aisle The center aisle of each chamber. When facing the presiding officer, Republicans usually sit to the right of the aisle, Democrats to the left.

Amendment A formal proposal to alter the text of a bill, resolution, amendment, motion, treaty, or some other text. Technically, it is a motion. An amendment may strike out (eliminate) part of a text, insert new text, or strike out and insert—that is, replace all or part of the text with new text.

Amendments are voted on in the same manner as a bill or other motions. Conference reports and certain motions are not amendable. The texts of amendments considered on the floor are printed in full in the *Congressional Record*.

Amendment in the Nature of a Substitute Usually, an amendment to replace the entire text of a measure. It strikes out everything after the enacting clause and inserts a version that may be somewhat, substantially, or entirely different.

Amendments Between the Houses The basic method for reconciling House and Senate differences on a measure is passing it back and forth between them until both have agreed to identical language by means of amendments. The method is used routinely for relatively noncontroversial measures and sometimes for major legislation that must be passed quickly.

Amendments in Disagreement Amendments in dispute between the houses. A conference committee is required to deal only with these amendments, and its conference report may contain recommendations concerning only those amendments on which it has reached agreement. Amendments on which the conference committee is unable to agree are presented to the houses as still in disagreement. After a house agrees to the conference report, the majority manager offers motions to dispose of the amendments in disagreement, either one at a time or en bloc.

Annual Authorization Legislation that authorizes appropriations for a single fiscal year and usually for a specific amount. Under the rules of the authorization-appropriation process, an annually authorized agency or program must be reauthorized each year if it is to receive appropriations for that year. Sometimes Congress fails to enact the reauthorization but nevertheless provides appropriations to continue the program, circumventing the rules by one means or another.

Appeal A member's formal challenge of a ruling or decision by the presiding officer. On appeal, a house or a committee may overturn the ruling by majority vote. The right of appeal ensures the body against arbitrary control by the chair.

Apportionment The action, after each decennial census, of allocating the number of members in the House of Representatives to each state. By law, the total number of House members (not counting delegates and a resident commissioner) is fixed at 435. The number allotted to each state is based approximately on its proportion of the nation's total population. Since the Constitution guarantees each state one representative no matter how small its population, exact proportional distribution is virtually impossible. The mathematical formula currently used to determine the apportionment is called the Method of Equal Proportions.

Appropriated Entitlement An entitlement program, such as food stamps or veterans' pensions, that is funded through annual appropriations rather than by a permanent appropriation. Because such an entitlement law requires the government to provide eligible recipients the benefits to which they are entitled, whatever the cost, Congress must appropriate the necessary funds.

Appropriation (1) Legislative language that permits a federal agency to incur obligations and make payments from the Treasury for specified purposes, usually during a specified period of time. (2) The specific amount of money made available by such language.

The Constitution prohibits payments from the Treasury except "in Consequence of Appropriations made by Law." With some exceptions, the rules of both houses forbid consideration of appropriations for purposes that are unauthorized in law or of appropriation amounts larger than those authorized in law.

The House of Representatives claims the exclusive right to originate appropriation bills—a claim the Senate denies in theory but accepts in practice. Consequently, the Senate Appropriations Committee usually waits for the arrival of a bill passed by the House and then reports it with whatever amendments it chooses.

Appropriation Limitation In budgetary parlance, a provision in an appropriations act establishing the maximum amount that may be obligated or spent for specified purposes.

Approval Terminology Congressional terms of approval differ according to the matter under consideration. Bills and joint resolutions are "passed," whereas simple resolutions, amendments, and most motions are "agreed to." Concurrent resolutions and amendments of the other house are "agreed to" or "concurred in." Conference reports are "adopted," points of order and rulings of the chair are "sustained," and the yeas and nays and engrossment and third reading are "ordered." When a motion for the previous question is agreed to, the previous question is said to be "ordered."

Arrest of Absent Members When a quorum is not present in a house, the Constitution authorizes it "to compel the Attendance of absent Members, in such Manner and under such Penalties as each House may provide." Under that authority, the rules of both houses permit the arrest of absent members under prescribed circumstances.

Assignments The committees and subcommittees on which a member serves.

At-Large Elected by and representing an entire state instead of a district within a state. The term usually refers to a representative rather than to a senator.

August Adjournment A congressional adjournment during the month of August in odd-numbered years, required by the Legislative Reorganization Act of 1970. The law instructs the two houses to adjourn for a period of at least thirty days before the second day after Labor Day, unless Congress provides otherwise or if, on July 31, a state of war exists by congressional declaration.

Authorization (1) A statutory provision that establishes or continues a federal agency, activity, or program for a fixed or indefinite period of time. It may also establish policies and restrictions and deal with organizational and administrative matters.

(2) A statutory provision that authorizes appropriations for an agency, activity, or program. The appropriations may be authorized for one year, several years, or an indefinite period of time, and the authorization may be for a specific amount of money or an indefinite amount ("such sums as may be necessary"). Authorizations of specific amounts are construed as ceilings on the amounts that subsequently may be appropriated in an appropriation bill, but not as minimums; either house may appropriate lesser amounts or nothing at all.

Authorization-Appropriation Process The two-stage procedural system that the rules of each house require for establishing and funding federal agencies and programs: first, enactment of authorizing legislation that creates or continues an agency or program; second, enactment of appropriations legislation that provides funds for the authorized agency or program.

The rules and precedents of the House establish four basic prohibitions: (1) no appropriation without an authorization in law, (2) no authorizing language in a general appropriation bill, (3) no appropriation in an authorizing measure, and (4) no appropriation larger than the amount, if any, specified in the authorization.

The Senate's rules differ from those of the House in several ways. They permit appropriations for authorizations the Senate has previously passed in the same session of Congress, not only for those enacted into law as the House requires. Furthermore, the Senate permits appropriations for unauthorized purposes if proposed by its Appropriations Committee, by any committee with jurisdiction over that purpose, or by any senator if the appropriation appears in the president's budget estimates. The Senate also allows appropriations in authorizing measures. In all other respects, the Senate's prohibitions are the same as those in the House. And both houses agree that Congress may appropriate less than the authorized amount or no amount at all.

To protect itself from the Senate's more liberal interpretation of the process, the House prohibits its conference managers from agreeing to (1) Senate amendments that violate the House's interpretation of authorized appropriations, or (2) appropriations in measures other than general appropriation bills. Although the conferees may agree to such provisions with the prior permission of the House, they ordinarily circumvent the rule by reporting the provisions as amendments in technical disagreement.

The rules of this process are enforced only when members raise points of order against potential violations. Moreover, one or more of the prohibitions may be waived, and often are, by unanimous consent, suspension of the rules, or, in the House, by a special rule.

The historical rationale for the process has been to prevent the delay of appropriation bills caused by disputes over substantive policy. However, such disputes still arise because the houses often circumvent the rules of the process.

Automatic Roll Call Under a House rule, the automatic ordering of the yeas and nays when a quorum is not present on a voice or division vote and a member objects to the vote on that ground. It is not permitted in the Committee of the Whole.

B

Backdoor Spending Authority Authority to incur obligations that evades the normal congressional appropriations process because it is provided in legislation other than appropriation acts. The most common forms are borrowing authority, contract authority, and entitlement authority. From the perspective of the appropriations committees, funding by these forms of spending authority slips away from their control through legislative back doors.

Balanced Budget Loosely, a budget with a surplus rather than a deficit. In governmental accounting terms, a budget in which anticipated or actual total revenues equal anticipated or actual total expenditures. Conversely, an unbalanced budget is one in which expenditures exceed revenues, or vice versa.

Balanced Budget Amendment A proposal for a constitutional amendment mandating that federal expenditures not exceed federal revenues in any fiscal year.

Baseline A projection of the levels of federal spending, revenues, and the resulting budgetary surpluses or deficits for the upcoming and subsequent fiscal years, taking into account laws enacted to date and assuming no new policy decisions. It provides a benchmark for measuring the budgetary effects of proposed changes in federal revenues or spending, assuming certain economic conditions. Baseline projections are prepared by the Congressional Budget Office.

Bicameral Consisting of two houses or chambers. Congress is a bicameral legislature whose two houses have an equal role in enacting legislation.

Bill The term for the chief vehicle Congress uses for enacting laws. Bills that originate in the House of Representatives are designated as H.R., those in the Senate as S., followed by a number assigned in the order in which they are introduced during a two-year Congress. A bill becomes a law if passed in identical language by both houses and signed by the president, or passed over his veto, or if the president fails to sign it within ten days after he has received it while Congress is in session.

Bill of Attainder An act of a legislature finding a person guilty of treason or a felony. The Constitution prohibits the passage of such a bill by Congress or any state legislature.

Bill Time Time for debate usually controlled by the majority and minority floor managers of a measure under a Senate unanimous consent agreement.

Bills and Resolutions Introduced Members formally present measures to their respective houses by delivering them to a clerk in the chamber when their house is in session. Both houses permit any number of members to join in introducing a bill or resolution. The first member listed on the measure is the sponsor; the other members listed are its cosponsors.

Bills and Resolutions Referred After a bill or resolution is introduced, it is normally sent to one or more committees that have jurisdiction over its subject, as defined by House and Senate rules and precedents. Officially, the Speaker refers measures in the House; the president of the Senate or president pro tempore refers measures in the Senate. In practice, those officers delegate the function to their parliamentarians, intervening only to deal with disputed referrals.

Bipartisan Committee A committee with an equal number of members from each political party. The House Committee on Standards of Official

Conduct and the Senate Select Committee on Ethics are the only bipartisan permanent full committees.

Bipartisan Measure A measure introduced or supported by members of both political parties, sometimes by both party leaders. When those leaders, sometimes joined by the president, agree that an issue is of such importance that they are willing to set aside normal considerations of partisan advantage, majorities in both houses usually vote for such a measure.

Body A term members in both the House and Senate use when referring to the other house, as in "the other body," or when referring to their own house, as in "this body." The Senate is often called the "upper body," the House the "lower body," terms disliked by many senior representatives and rarely heard on the floor of either chamber.

Borrowing Authority Statutory authority permitting a federal agency, such as the Export-Import Bank, to borrow money from the public or the Treasury to finance its operations. It is a form of backdoor spending. To bring such spending under the control of the congressional appropriation process, the Congressional Budget Act requires that new borrowing authority shall be effective only to the extent and in such amounts as are provided in appropriations acts.

Budget A detailed statement of actual or anticipated revenues and expenditures during an accounting period. For the national government, the period is the federal fiscal year (October 1-September 30). The budget usually refers to the president's budget submission to Congress early each calendar year. The president's budget estimates federal government income and spending for the upcoming fiscal year and contains detailed recommendations for appropriation, revenue, and other legislation. Congress is not required to accept or even vote directly on the president's proposals, and it often revises the president's budget extensively.

Budget Act Common name for the Congressional Budget and Impoundment Control Act of 1974, which established the basic procedures of the current congressional budget process; created the House and Senate budget committees; and enacted procedures for reconciliation, deferrals, and rescissions.

Budget Allocation (1) In congressional budgeting usage, the portion of budget authority, outlays, and other resources from a budget resolution that is assigned to a committee that has jurisdiction over such resources.

The Congressional Budget Act of 1974 requires the distribution of allocations to all appropriate committees in each house, and it also directs each committee to subdivide its allocation among its programs or subcommittees.

(2) In executive branch budgeting parlance, the budget authority and other resources transferred from one agency's account to another agency to carry out the purposes of the parent account.

Budget and Accounting Act of 1921 The law that, for the first time, authorized the president to submit to Congress an annual budget for the entire federal government. Prior to the act, most federal agencies sent their budget requests to the appropriate congressional committees without review by the president. The act also established a Bureau of the Budget (renamed the Office of Management and Budget [OMB] in 1970) to assist the president in preparing a budget and the General Accounting Office (GAO), headed by the comptroller general of the United States, to act as the principal auditing agency of the federal government.

Budget Authority Generally, the amount of money that may be spent or obligated by a government agency or for a government program or activity. Technically, it is statutory authority to enter into obligations that normally result in outlays. The main forms of budget authority are appropriations, borrowing authority, and contract authority. Congress may make budget authority available for only one year, several years, or an indefinite period, and it may specify definite or indefinite amounts.

Budget Authority Balances The amount of budget authority provided in previous fiscal years that had not been spent by the start of the current fiscal year.

Budget Enforcement Act of 1990 An act that revised the sequestration process of the Gramm-Rudman-Hollings Act of 1985, replaced its fixed deficit targets with adjustable ones, established discretionary spending limits for fiscal years 1991 through 1995, instituted pay-as-you-go rules to enforce deficit neutrality on revenue and mandatory spending legislation, and reformed the budget and accounting rules for federal credit activities. Unlike Gramm-Rudman-Hollings, the 1990 act emphasized restraints on legislated changes in taxes and spending instead of fixed deficit limits.

Budget Process (1) In Congress, the procedural system it uses (a) to approve an annual concurrent resolution on the budget that sets goals for aggregate and functional categories of federal expenditures, revenues, and the surplus or deficit for an upcoming fiscal year; and (b) to implement those goals in spending, revenue, and, if necessary, reconciliation and debt-limit legislation.

(2) In the executive branch, the process of formulating the president's annual budget, submitting it to Congress, defending it before congressional committees, implementing subsequent budget-related legislation, impounding or sequestering expenditures as permitted by law, auditing and evaluating programs, and compiling final budget data.

The Budget and Accounting Act of 1921 and the Congressional Budget and Impoundment Control Act of 1974 established the basic elements of the current budget process. Major revisions were enacted in the Gramm-Rudman-Hollings Act of 1985 and the Budget Enforcement Act of 1990.

Budget Receipts Monies collected by the government from the public generally and from premium payments by participants in certain social insurance programs. Collections from the general public consist primarily of taxes, but they also include court fines, certain license fees, deposits of earnings by the Federal Reserve System, and gifts.

Budget Resolution A concurrent resolution in which Congress establishes or revises its version of the federal budget's broad financial features for the upcoming fiscal year and several additional fiscal years. Like other concurrent resolutions, it does not have the force of law, but it provides the framework within which Congress subsequently considers revenue, spending, and other budget-implementing legislation.

The framework consists of two basic elements: (1) aggregate budget amounts (total revenues, new budget authority, outlays, loan obligations and loan guarantee commitments, deficit or surplus, and debt limit); and (2) subdivisions of the relevant aggregate amounts among the functional categories of the budget. The resolution also may contain reconciliation instructions to various committees. Although it does not allocate funds to specific programs or accounts, the budget committees' reports accompanying the resolution often discuss the major program assumptions underlying its functional amounts. Unlike those amounts, however, the assumptions are not binding on Congress.

Business The Constitution permits a house to "do business" only if a quorum is present, but it does not define "business." Consequently, each house, through its rules and precedents, has developed some implicit concepts of business that are similar and some that are not.

Both generally agree that business signifies a measure or matter that may be considered or is being considered, as in business on a calendar, legislative business, pending business, and unfinished business. With some differences, both agree that business also includes certain actions, such as approval of the *Journal*, offering of motions, referral of measures and communications, receipt of messages, and presentation of committee reports.

The House and Senate differ radically, however, on what constitutes the business that must be transacted between the time a quorum has been established and the time that a member may make a point of order that a quorum is no longer present. Under the Senate's precedents, almost any action is considered intervening business for that purpose. Under rules the House adopted during the 1970s, a member's right to make a point of no quorum is limited almost entirely to situations in which the chair has put a question to a vote. Implicitly, these House rules reduce its concept of intervening business to nearly the barest minimum.

By Request A designation indicating that a member has introduced a measure on behalf of the president, an executive agency, or a private individual or organization. Members often introduce such measures as a courtesy because neither the president nor any person other than a member of Congress can do so.

Byrd Rule Popular name of an amendment to the Congressional Budget Act that bars the inclusion of extraneous matter in any reconciliation legislation considered in the Senate. Its chief sponsor was Sen. Robert C. Byrd (D-W.Va).

C

Calendar A list of measures or other matters (most of them favorably reported by committees) that are eligible for floor consideration. The House has five calendars; the Senate has two. A place on a calendar does not guarantee consideration. Each house decides which measures and matters it will take up, when, and in what order, in accordance with its rules and practices.

Calendar Wednesday A House procedure that on Wednesdays permits its committees to bring up for floor consideration nonprivileged measures they have reported. It is primarily a method for circumventing the Rules Committee's refusal to report special rules granting privilege to those measures. The procedure is so cumbersome and susceptible to dilatory tactics, however, that committees rarely use it, and the call is normally dispensed with by unanimous consent. If unanimous consent is denied, it may be dispensed with by a two-thirds vote.

Calendars of the United States House of Representatives A publication that contains all the House calendars and other useful information about pending measures. It is published each day the House is in session.

Call of the Calendar (1) A procedure in which the measures on a calendar are called up for possible floor consideration in the order of their calendar numbers. The House consent and private calendars are called on days set aside for them in the rules. A Senate rule requires a call of its legislative calendar each legislative day after it concludes morning business. When called, a measure is considered if no one objects, and no senator may speak more than once and for no more than five minutes on the measure or on any amendment to it.

(2) An informal Senate practice, analogous to House consent calendar procedure, in which noncontroversial measures on the calendar are called up and passed without objection and with little or no debate.

Call Up To bring a measure or report to the floor for immediate consideration. Technically, only privileged business or business made in order by a special rule may be called up in the House and, if reported by a committee, only by an authorized member of the committee. The term is seldom used in the Senate, where immediate consideration of any business usually requires agreement to a motion to consider or to a unanimous consent request.

Cannon's Procedure in the House of Representatives A digest of leading House precedents and procedural terminology compiled by Clarence A. Cannon, a former unofficial House parliamentarian and later a House member and chairman of the Appropriations Committee. It is still a useful guide to House procedures and terminology, although it was last published in 1963 and is therefore outdated in some areas.

Cap The legal limit on new spending and budget authority in a discretionary appropriations category of the budget during a particular fiscal year. The Budget Enforcement Act of 1990 requires a sequester in a category if its cap is exceeded.

Casework Assistance to constituents who seek assistance in dealing with federal and local government agencies. Constituent service is a high priority in most members' offices. Caseworkers on members' staffs advise constituents about agency regulations and procedures, determine whether any complaints are justified, and try to persuade agencies to rectify errors or injustices. If an agency remains adamant or uncooperative, the member may take up the case himself. Most cases involve problems with Social Security benefits, veterans' benefits, and immigration.

Casting Vote The vice president's vote while presiding over the Senate. It may be cast only to break a tie vote, but the vice president is not required to vote.

Caucus (1) A common term for the official organization of each party in each house.

(2) The official title of the organization of House Democrats. House and Senate Republicans and Senate Democrats call their organizations "conferences."

(3) A term for an informal group of members who share legislative interests; some groups are referred to as legislative service organizations. Several of these use the term in their titles, such as the Arts Caucus, Black Caucus, Hispanic Caucus, Mushroom Caucus, Children's Caucus, and Crime Caucus.

Censure The strongest formal condemnation of a member for misconduct short of expulsion. A house usually adopts a resolution of censure to express its condemnation, after which the presiding officer reads its rebuke aloud to the member in the presence of his colleagues. Under a rule of the House Democratic Caucus, a censured Democratic representative loses his committee and subcommittee chairmanships for the remainder of that Congress.

The authority of Congress to censure stems from the constitutional provision permitting it to "punish its members for disorderly behavior."

Chair (1) The person presiding over a meeting, as in "the decision of the chair."

(2) The seat occupied by that person. To "take the chair" is to preside.

Chairman The presiding officer of a committee (including the Committee of the Whole), a subcommittee, or a task force. At meetings, the chairman preserves order, enforces the rules, recognizes members to speak or offer motions, and puts questions to a vote. The chairman of a committee or subcommittee usually appoints its staff and sets its agenda, subject to the panel's veto. A committee chairman is required to report measures approved by the committee, usually manages measures during floor consideration, and recommends members for appointment to conference committees.

Senate committee chairmen are invariably selected on the basis of seniority on the committee, but they may not chair more than one standing committee. House chairmen are chosen by their party's caucus or conference, usually on the basis of seniority, and they, too, may chair only one standing committee. Although chairmen are formally elected by their houses, they are always the nominees of the majority party.

Chamber The Capitol room in which a house of Congress normally holds its sessions. The chamber of the House of Representatives, officially called the Hall of the House, is considerably larger than that of the Senate because it must accommodate 435 representatives, 4 delegates, and 1 resident commissioner. Unlike the Senate chamber, members have no desks or assigned seats.

In both chambers, the floor slopes downward to the well in front of the presiding officer's raised desk. A chamber is often referred to as "the floor," as when members are said to be on or going to the floor.

Christmas Tree Bill Jargon for a bill adorned with amendments, many of them unrelated to the bill's subject, that provide benefits for interest groups, specific states, congressional districts, companies, and individuals. Such amendments are usually attached in the Senate where, unlike in the House, nongermane amendments are normally permitted, but both houses tend to add them to must-pass bills, such as debt ceiling increases and continuing resolutions, especially toward the end of an annual session of Congress.

Classes of Senators A class consists of the thirty-three or thirty-four senators elected to a six-year term in the same general election. Since the terms of approximately one-third of the senators expire every two years, there are three classes.

Clause (1) A special and separate provision in a measure or law, such as an enacting clause or resolving clause.

(2) In the House, the first subdivision of a standing rule: for example, Rule I, clause 1.

(3) A second subdivision of the Constitution.

Clean Bill After a House committee extensively amends a bill, it often assembles its amendments and what is left of the bill into a new measure that one or more of its members introduces as a "clean bill." The revised measure is assigned a new number.

Cleaves' Manual Short title for "Cleaves' Manual of the Law and Practices in Regard to Conferences and Conference Reports," usually published as a section of the *Senate Manual*. Although compiled in about 1900, most of the procedures it describes are still applicable today.

Clerk of the House An officer of the House of Representatives responsible principally for administrative support of the legislative process in the House. The clerk's former functions as chief administrative and budgetary officer were assigned to a director of non-legislative and financial services by a resolution agreed to on April 9, 1992. Invariably the candidate of the majority party, the clerk is elected by resolution at the beginning of each Congress and continues in office until a successor is chosen.

Clerk-Hire The personal staff to which a member is entitled. The clerk-hire allowance is the maximum amount of money available to a member to compensate his or her staff.

In the House, both the number of staff a member may hire and the allowance amount are established by law or resolution. The Senate sets no limit on the number of personal staff a senator may hire within the limits of the allowance, but senators from the more populous states are authorized larger sums.

Cloakrooms Two rooms with access to the rear of each chamber's floor, one for each party's members, where members may confer privately, sit quietly, or have a snack.

Closed Hearing A hearing closed to the public and the press. A House committee may close its hearing only if it determines that disclosure of the testimony to be taken would endanger national security, violate any law, or tend to defame, degrade, or incriminate any person. The Senate has a similar rule. Both houses require roll-call votes in open session to close a hearing.

Closed Rule A special rule reported from the House Rules Committee that prohibits amendments to a measure or that only permits amendments offered by the reporting committee.

Cloture A Senate procedure that limits further consideration of a pending proposal to thirty hours in order to end a filibuster.

Sixteen senators must first sign and submit a cloture motion to the presiding officer. One hour after the Senate meets on the second calendar day thereafter, the chair puts the motion to a yea-and-nay vote following a live quorum call. If three-fifths of all senators (sixty if there are no vacancies) vote for the motion, the Senate must take final action on the clotured proposal by the end of the thirty hours of consideration and may consider no other business until it takes that action. Cloture on a proposal to amend the Senate's standing rules requires approval by two-thirds of the senators present and voting. The vote on cloture occurs after the presiding officer asks the question: "Is it the sense of the Senate that the debate shall be brought to a close?"

Once cloture is invoked, each senator may speak for a total of no more than one hour.

Senators may yield all or part of their hour to one of the floor managers or floor leaders who may in turn yield that time to other senators, but each manager and leader may be yielded no more than two hours.

No dilatory amendments or motions are allowed, and all debate and amendments must be germane. Only amendments filed before the cloture vote may be considered, but no senator may call up more than two amendments until every other senator has had an opportunity to do so. Printed amendments that have been available for at least twenty-four hours are not read when called up.

Code of Official Conduct A House rule that bans certain actions by House members, officers, and employees; requires them to conduct themselves in ways that "reflect creditably" on the House; and orders them to adhere to the spirit and the letter of House rules and those of its committees.

The code's provisions govern the receipt of outside compensation, gifts, and honoraria, and the use of campaign funds; prohibit members from using their clerk-hire allowance to pay anyone who does not perform duties commensurate with that pay; forbids discrimination in members' hiring or treatment of employees on the grounds of race, color, religion, sex, handicap, age, or national origin; orders members convicted of a crime who might be punished by imprisonment of two or more years not to participate in committee business or vote on the floor until exonerated or reelected; and restricts employees' contact with federal agencies on matters in which they have a significant financial interest. The Senate's rules contain some similar prohibitions.

College of Cardinals A popular term for the subcommittee chairmen of the appropriations committees, reflecting their influence over appropriation measures. The chairmen of the full appropriations committees are sometimes referred to as popes.

Colloquy A formal conversational exchange between members during floor proceedings. The device is often used to obtain information or to put mutual understandings about the intent of a measure, a provision, or an amendment into the *Congressional Record,* thereby establishing legislative history for the guidance of executive officials and the courts. Legislative history colloquies are usually prepared and agreed to in advance by the members involved.

Comity The practice of maintaining mutual courtesy and civility between the two houses in their dealings with each other and in members' speeches on the floor. Although the practice is largely governed by long-established customs, a House rule explicitly cautions its members not to characterize any Senate action or inaction, refer to individual senators except under certain circumstances, or quote from Senate proceedings except to make legislative history on a measure.

The Senate has no rule on the subject, but references to the House have been held out of order on several occasions. Generally, the houses do not interfere with each other's appropriations, although minor conflicts sometimes occur. A refusal to receive a message from the other house has also been held to violate the practice of comity.

Commit To send or return to a committee. As a practical matter, the terms "commit," "recommit," and "refer" are essentially synonymous.

Committee A panel of members elected or appointed to perform some service or function for its parent body. Congress has four types of committees: standing, special or select, joint, and, in the House, a Committee of the Whole.

Except for the Committee of the Whole, committees conduct investigations, make studies, issue reports and recommendations, and, in the case of standing committees, review and prepare measures on their assigned subjects for action by their respective houses. Most committees divide their work among several subcommittees or, in some cases, task forces, but only the full committee may submit reports or measures to its house or to Congress. With rare exceptions, the majority party in a house holds a majority of the seats on its committees, and their chairmen are also from that party.

Modern committees vary in size from about twelve to almost seventy members in the House and from six to about thirty members in the Senate. The Appropriations Committee is always the largest standing committee in each house. Every committee is entitled to staff, offices, office equipment and supplies, and funds for other expenses.

Committee Assignments The committees on which a member serves. Although each house formally makes the assignments to its committees, it invariably ratifies the recommendations of the party organizations.

Both parties consider a number of factors in making assignments, including seniority, experience, background, ideology, and the special interests of a member's district or state. In addition, the rules of the party organizations and the houses attempt to ensure an equitable number of assignments for each member and an equitable distribution of assignments to important committees. With rare exceptions, each representative is assigned to at least one standing committee; most representatives sit on two standing committees, and a few serve on three. Senators must serve on at least two standing committees but many sit on three or four. In addition, many members in both houses are assigned to select and joint committees.

The rules of the House Democratic Caucus divide committees into three classes: exclusive, major, and nonmajor. A Democrat who sits on an exclusive committee—Appropriations, Ways and Means, or Rules—may not serve on any other standing committee except Budget or House Administration. No Democrat may serve on more than one of the eight major committees, on more than two of the ten nonmajor committees, or on more than one major plus one nonmajor committee. In practice, however, the caucus often grants waivers from one or more of these limitations.

House Republicans follow the same general categorization. However, their rankings of committees differ by largely depending on committee vacancies and the relative interest of Republican members in serving on each particular committee.

Both Senate party conferences also designate a few committees as exclusive, but only in the sense that no senator may serve on more than one of them. In addition, the standing rules divide all committees into three classes for assignment purposes. The first, often called class A, consists of twelve standing committees, and each senator *must* serve on two of them, but no more than two. Despite the limitation, the Senate often grants waivers for many senators; in the 102d Congress, twenty-three senators were assigned to three class A committees. Class B committees consist of four standing committees, two select committees, and one joint committee. A senator *may* sit on one of them, but no more than one. Class C committees consist of two select committees and three joint committees. With certain exceptions, a senator may sit on any number of them.

Committee Calendar A list of all measures referred to a particular committee during a Congress, its actions on them, and chamber action on those it has reported.

Committee Jurisdiction The legislative subjects and other functions assigned to a committee by rule, precedent, resolution, or statute. A committee's title usually indicates the general scope of its jurisdiction but often fails to mention other significant subjects assigned to it.

Because each house has a relatively small number of standing committees, many of them have immense jurisdictions, which is one reason for the creation of numerous subcommittees.

Committee of the Whole Common name of the Committee of the Whole House on the State of the Union, a committee consisting of all members of the House of Representatives. Measures from the union calendar must be considered in the Committee of the Whole before the House officially completes action on them; the committee often considers other major bills as well. A quorum of the committee is 100, and it meets in the House chamber under a chairman appointed by the Speaker.

The committee's proceedings begin with general debate on the measure for a period of time previously ordered by the House, usually from one hour to several hours. That time is controlled by, and equally divided between, the majority and minority floor managers, but when more than one committee reports on the measure the time is distributed among them. The committee then considers amendments under the five-minute rule. Debate on amendments may be closed or limited by majority vote on a nondebatable motion. If the committee does not complete its deliberations on a measure in one day, it can meet again on subsequent days.

The committee operates partly under House rules explicitly governing its procedures and partly under practices of the House that implicitly apply to the committee, but both are often modified by special rules from the Rules Committee. In any case, the Committee of the Whole does not allow the yeas and nays or motions to adjourn, lay on the table, recess, recommit, reconsider, or for the previous question.

When the committee finishes with a measure, it rises and reports back to the House by recommending that the bill be passed with whatever amendments the committee has approved. The special rule on the measure bans additional floor amendments at this stage and prohibits debate on the measure, on the committee's amendments to it, and on all the necessary steps to passage. However, any member may demand a separate vote on any amendment reported by the Committee of the Whole.

The Senate no longer uses a Committee of the Whole. It abolished such proceedings on bills and joint resolutions in 1930 and stopped its use for the consideration of treaties in 1986.

Procedures in the Committee of the Whole expedite consideration of legislation because of its smaller quorum requirement, its ban on certain motions, and its five-minute rule for debate on amendments. Those procedures usually permit more members to offer amendments and participate in the debate on a measure than is normally possible when the measure is considered in the House, where the hour rule, the previous question motion, and the ban on dilatory motions can be far more restrictive.

Committee on Committees A political party committee that assigns party members to positions on standing committees and most select committees in its house, subject to approval by the party organization and pro forma election by the chamber. Ordinarily, the committee only fills vacant positions, adhering to the custom that members should not be removed from their assignments without their consent.

Only the Republicans in both houses give their panels the formal name of "Committee on Committees." House Democrats assign the function to their Steering and Policy Committee, Senate Democrats to their Steering Committee.

Committee Print A document printed either for the use of a committee or for other informational purposes. Most committees publish their rules in committee prints.

Committee Ratios The ratios of majority to minority party members on committees. By custom, the ratios of most committees reflect party strength in their respective houses as closely as possible. In the House, however, the Appropriations, Budget, Rules, and Ways and Means committees often have disproportionate ratios to ensure firm majority party control.

Committee Report on a Measure A document submitted by a committee to report a measure to its parent chamber. Customarily, the report explains the measure's purpose, describes provisions and any amendments recommended by the committee, and presents arguments for its approval. The text of the committee's amendments appears at the beginning of the document. Reports are designated S. Rpt. in the Senate, H. Rpt. in the House; both are numbered sequentially in the order of filing during a Congress.

Committee Veto A procedure that requires an executive department or agency to submit certain proposed policies, programs, or action to designated committees for review before implementing them. Before 1983, when the Supreme Court declared that a legislative veto is unconstitutional, these provisions permitted committees to veto the proposals. They no longer do so, and the term is now something of a misnomer. Nevertheless, agencies usually take the pragmatic approach of trying to reach a consensus with the committees before carrying out their proposals, especially when an appropriations committee is involved.

Companion Bills Identical or similar bills introduced in both houses.

Comptroller General of the United States The head of the General Accounting Office. The comptroller general is appointed to a fifteen-year term by the president, but only Congress can remove him from office before the end of his appointed term.

Concur Agree to an amendment of the other house, either by adopting a motion to concur in that amendment or by a motion to concur with an amendment to that amendment.

Concurrent Resolution A resolution that requires approval by both houses but is not sent to the president for his signature and therefore cannot have the force of law.

Concurrent resolutions deal with the prerogatives or internal affairs of Congress as a whole. Designated H. Con. Res. in the House and S. Con. Res. in the Senate, they are numbered consecutively in each house in their order of introduction during a two-year Congress.

Conditional Adjournment An adjournment of Congress for a specified period of more than three days with the proviso that the Speaker of the House and the Senate's president pro tempore (or sometimes its majority leader) may reconvene Congress at an earlier date.

Conferees A common title for managers, the members from each house appointed to a conference committee. The Senate usually authorizes its presiding officer to appoint its conferees. The Speaker appoints House conferees, and under a rule adopted in 1993, can remove conferees "at any time after an original appointment" and also appoint additional conferees at any time. Conferees are expected to support the positions of their houses despite their personal views, but in practice this is not always the case.

The party ratios of conferees generally reflect the ratios in their houses.

Invariably, most conferees—often all of them—are members of the committee that reported the measure.

Each house may appoint as many conferees as it pleases. House conferees often outnumber their Senate colleagues; however, each house has only one vote in a conference, so the size of its delegation is immaterial.

Conference (1) A formal meeting or series of meetings between members representing each house to reconcile House and Senate differences on a measure (occasionally several measures). Also, a common reference to a conference committee.

A conference is permitted to deal only with matters in disagreement between the houses. It may not change language that both have previously approved, nor may it insert a subject not dealt with in either the House or the Senate version of the measure.

Since one house cannot require the other to agree to its proposals, the conference usually reaches agreement by compromise.

When a conference completes action on a measure, or as much action as appears possible, it sends its recommendations to both houses in the form of a conference report, accompanied by an explanatory statement.

(2) The official title of the organization of all Democrats or Republicans in the Senate and of all Republicans in the House.

Conference Committee A temporary joint committee formed for the purpose of resolving differences between the houses on a measure or, occasionally, several measures. Major and controversial legislation usually require conference committee action. Voting in a conference committee is by house as determined by a majority vote of its conferees, not by individuals. Consequently, a committee decision must be affirmed by a majority of the conferees from each house.

Conference Report A document submitted to both houses that contains a conference committee's agreements for resolving their differences on a measure. It must be signed by a majority of the conferees from each house and must be accompanied by an explanatory statement.

Both houses prohibit amendments to a conference report and require it to be accepted or rejected in its entirety.

Confirmation A Senate action approving a nomination submitted by the president.

Congress (1) The national legislature of the United States, consisting of the House of Representatives and the Senate.

(2) The national legislature in office during a two-year period. Congresses are numbered sequentially; thus, the 1st Congress of 1789-1791 and the 102d Congress of 1991-1993. Before 1935, the two-year period began on the first Monday in December of odd-numbered years. Since then it has extended from January of an odd-numbered year through noon on January 3 of the next odd-numbered year. A Congress usually holds two annual sessions, but some have had three sessions and the 67th Congress had four. When a Congress expires, measures die if they have not yet been enacted.

Congressional Budget and Impoundment Control Act of 1974 The law that established the basic elements of the congressional budget process, the House and Senate budget committees, the Congressional Budget Office, and the procedures for congressional review of impoundments in the form of rescissions and deferrals proposed by the president. The budget process consists of procedures for coordinating congressional revenue and spending decisions made in separate tax, appropriations, and legislative measures. The impoundment provisions were intended to give Congress greater control over executive branch actions that delay or prevent the spending of funds provided by Congress.

Congressional Budget Office (CBO) A congressional support agency created by the Congressional Budget and Impoundment Control Act of 1974 to provide nonpartisan budgetary information and analysis to Congress and its committees.

Congressional Directory The official who's who of Congress, usually published during the first session of a two-year Congress. Among other features, it contains brief biographies of all members and their committee assignments, office locations and telephone numbers. The *Directory* has been published by Congress continuously since 1821.

Congressional District The geographical area represented by a single member of the House of Representatives. For states with only one representative, the entire state is a congressional district.

Congressional Record The daily, printed, and substantially verbatim account of proceedings in both the House and Senate chambers. Extraneous materials submitted by members appear in a section titled "Extensions of Remarks." A "Daily Digest" appendix contains highlights of the day's floor and committee action plus a list of committee meetings and floor agendas for the next day's session.

Congressional Research Service (CRS) A department of the Library of Congress whose staff provide nonpartisan, objective analyses and information on virtually any subject to committees, members, and staff of Congress. Established in 1917 as the Legislative Reference Service, it is the oldest congressional support agency.

Congressional Terms of Office A term normally begins on January 3 of the year following a general election and runs two years for representatives and six years for senators.

Consent Calendar A House calendar, and the procedures associated with it, used to expedite passage of noncontroversial legislation.

Consider To take up a measure, motion, or matter for the purpose of acting on it. In most cases, the Senate uses a debatable motion to proceed to consider a bill or resolution and a nondebatable motion to proceed to the consideration of executive business.

Constitutional Rules Constitutional provisions that prescribe procedures for Congress. In addition to certain types of votes required in particular situations, they include: (1) the House chooses its Speaker, the Senate its president pro tempore, and both houses their officers; (2) each house requires a majority quorum to conduct business; (3) less than a majority may adjourn from day to day and compel the attendance of absent members; (4) neither house may adjourn for more than three days without the consent of the other; (5) each house must keep a journal; (6) the yeas and nays are ordered when supported by one-fifth of the members present; (7) all revenue-raising bills must originate in the House, but the Senate may propose amendments to them; (8) the procedure in the House for electing a president; (9) the procedure in the Senate for electing a vice president; (10) the procedure for filling a vacancy in the office of vice president; (11) the procedure for overriding a presidential veto.

Constitutional Votes Constitutional provisions that require certain votes or voting methods in specific situations. They include: (1) the yeas and nays at the desire of one-fifth of the members present; (2) a two-thirds vote by the yeas and nays to override a veto; (3) a two-thirds vote by one house to expel one of its members and by both houses to propose a constitutional amendment; (4) a two-thirds vote of senators present to convict one of its members of impeachment charges and to consent to ratification of treaties; (5) a two-thirds vote in each house to remove political disabilities from persons who have engaged in insurrection or rebellion or given aid or comfort to the enemies of the United States; (6) a majority vote in each house to fill a vacancy in the office of vice president; (7) a majority vote of all states to elect a president in the House of Representatives when no candidate receives a majority of the electoral votes; (8) a majority vote of all senators when the Senate elects a vice president under the same circumstances; (9) the casting vote of the vice president in case of tie votes in the Senate.

Contempt of Congress Willful obstruction of the proper functions of Congress. Most frequently, it is a refusal to obey a subpoena to appear and testify before a committee or to produce documents demanded by it. Such obstruction is a misdemeanor and persons cited for contempt are subject to prosecution in federal courts.

Contingency Appropriation An appropriation that becomes available only if some specified future action occurs. Such an action might be submission of a report by a federal official, settlement of litigation, enactment of an authorization, or enactment of some other specified law.

Contingent Fund A sum of money appropriated annually to each house for expenditures that are not separately authorized and appropriated. Each house uses its fund for a variety of miscellaneous purposes.

Contingent Liability A conditional commitment by the government, such as a loan guarantee, price guarantee, or bank deposit insurance, that may become an actual liability in the future and require the expenditure of federal monies because of an event beyond the government's control, such as a bank failure.

Continuing Body A characterization of the Senate on the theory that it continues from Congress to Congress and has existed continuously since it first convened in 1789. The rationale for the theory is that under the system of staggered six-year terms for senators, the terms of only about one-third of them expire after each Congress and, therefore, a quorum of the Senate is always in office. Consequently, the Senate, unlike the House, does not have to adopt its rules at the beginning of each Congress because those rules continue from one Congress to the next. This makes it extremely difficult for the Senate to change its rules against the opposition of a determined minority because those rules require a two-thirds vote of the senators present and voting to invoke cloture on a proposed rules change.

Continuing Business By rule or practice, all measures introduced in a two-year Congress and still awaiting final action at the end of an annual or special session of that Congress continue to be available for action during any subsequent session of that Congress. Measures that have not been passed by the end of a Congress die but may be reintroduced in the next Congress.

Continuing Resolution (CR) A joint resolution that provides funds to continue the operation of federal agencies and programs at the beginning of a new fiscal year if their annual appropriation bills have not yet been enacted; also called continuing appropriations. Enacted shortly before or after the new fiscal year begins, the first continuing resolution usually makes funds available for a specified period; additional resolutions are often needed after the first expires.

Contract Authority Statutory authority permitting an agency to enter into contracts or incur other obligations even though it has not received an appropriation to pay for them. Congress must eventually fund them because the government is legally liable for such payments.

Controllable Expenditures Federal spending that is permitted but not mandated by existing authorization law and therefore may be adjusted by congressional action in appropriation bills.

Cordon Rule A Senate rule requiring that a committee report on a bill or joint resolution contain the text of any statutory provision it proposes to repeal and also a comparative print showing the changes in existing law that would be made by the language proposed by the committee, using typographical devices such as stricken-through type or italics. Named after its sponsor, Sen. Guy Cordon (R-Ore.), the rule is analogous to the Ramseyer Rule in the House.

Correction of Remarks Members are permitted to correct the transcripts of their remarks spoken on the floor or during committee meetings before they are printed. Once floor remarks have been published in the daily edition of the *Congressional Record,* they may be corrected in the permanent *Record* by unanimous consent.

Correcting Recorded Votes The rules of both houses prohibit members from changing their votes after a vote result has been announced. Nevertheless, the Senate permits its members to withdraw or change their votes, by unanimous consent, immediately after the announcement. In rare instances, senators have been granted unanimous consent to change their votes several days or weeks after the announcement.

Votes tallied by the electronic voting system in the House may not be changed. But when a vote actually given is not recorded during an oral call of the roll, a member may demand a correction as a matter of right. On all other alleged errors in a recorded vote, the Speaker determines whether the circumstances justify a change.

Cosponsor A member who has joined one or more other members to sponsor a measure.

Cost Estimates Estimates that provide data used in determining whether the budget resolution's requirements, the caps on discretionary spending categories, the rules on deficit neutrality, or the statutory limits on annual deficits have been violated. In both houses, a committee's report on a measure must include an estimate of its cost "in the fiscal year in which it is reported and in each of the five fiscal years following" or for the authorized duration of any program in the measure, if less than five years.

Counting a Quorum In the House, the Speaker and the chairman of the Committee of the Whole are authorized to count members to determine whether a quorum is present. They count all members in sight in the chamber and in the cloakrooms, and their count may not be appealed. Normally, the Senate does not permit a count to determine whether a quorum is present. Under cloture, however, the presiding officer may count senators to reaffirm that a quorum is still present so that he may rule out a dilatory request for a quorum call.

Credit Authority Authority granted to an agency to incur direct loan obligations or to make loan guarantee commitments.

Credit Budget The levels of new federal direct loan obligations and new loan guarantee commitments that appear in a budget resolution.

They are the basis for limitations on direct and guaranteed loans in appropriations acts.

Credit Subsidy Cost The estimated long-term cost of a direct loan or loan guarantee to the federal government.

C-SPAN Cable-Satellite Public Affairs Network, which provides live, gavel-to-gavel coverage of Senate floor proceedings on one cable television channel and coverage of House floor proceedings on another channel. C-SPAN also televises important committee hearings in both Houses. Each house also transmits its televised proceedings directly to congressional offices.

Current Services Estimates Executive branch estimates of the anticipated costs of federal programs and operations for the next and future fiscal years at existing levels of service and assuming no new initiatives or changes in existing law. The president submits these estimates to Congress with his annual budget.

D

Daily Digest A section of the *Congressional Record* summarizing the day's floor and committee actions in each house, with page references to the verbatim accounts of floor actions. It also lists the measures scheduled for action during each house's next meeting and the announcements of upcoming committee meetings.

Dance of the Swans and the Ducks A whimsical description of the gestures some members use in connection with a request for a recorded vote, especially in the House. When a member wants his colleagues to stand in support of the request, he moves his hands and arms in a "gentle upward motion resembling the beginning flight of a graceful swan." When he wants his colleagues to remain seated in order to avoid such a vote, he moves his hands and arms "in a vigorous downward motion resembling a diving duck."

Debate In congressional parlance, speeches delivered during consideration of a measure, motion, or other matter, as distinguished from speeches in other parliamentary situations, such as one-minute and special order speeches when no business is pending.

Virtually all debate in the House of Representatives is under some kind of time limitation. Most debate in the Senate is unlimited; that is, a senator, once recognized, may speak for as long as he chooses, unless the Senate invokes cloture.

Debate-Ending Motion A motion whose adoption normally ends discussion on a pending matter immediately. Such a motion is not debatable and is adopted by majority vote because its purpose is to expedite the proceedings.

The House has two debate-ending motions: the previous question, permitted when the House is sitting in its legislative capacity as the House of Representatives; and a motion to close debate in the Committee of the Whole. The previous question immediately shuts off debate only if some debate has already occurred; if not, forty minutes of debate are permitted. Another exception is allowed after the Committee of the Whole has voted to close debate; amendments printed in the *Congressional Record* may be debated for ten minutes each.

A third debate-ending motion—to lay on the table—is available in both houses, but not in the Committee of the Whole. However, it ends debate by killing the proposal to which it is applied and, in the House, the underlying measure.

Except for the motion to lay on the table, the Senate, strictly speaking, permits no debate-ending motions; cloture sets a time limit on further consideration rather than ending debate immediately.

Debt Limit The maximum amount of outstanding federal public debt permitted by law.

Decorum Orderly and courteous behavior and speech in a parliamentary body. As enforced in the U.S. Congress, orderly procedure requires that only one member may speak at a time, the member may speak only when recognized, and that the member may not be interrupted without his consent unless a rule or practice of the chamber has been violated.

Both houses of Congress frown on loud conversations, hissing, jeering, and similar disruptive behavior while a member is speaking. Both houses permit points of order against such behavior and authorize their presiding officers to call their chambers and individual members to order. In addition, a House rule prohibits members from passing between the chair and a member who is speaking, and it is also considered impolite to walk near the member who is speaking.

Both houses also attempt to enforce civility in debate. Inevitably, Congress often deals with controversial and emotional issues that strain members' tempers and inflame their passions. To minimize personal confrontations that might disrupt their proceedings, both houses require members to address the chair, and only the chair, when they are recognized. They may not speak directly to other members; may refer to them only in the third person; and are prohibited from engaging in personalities or imputing unworthy motives or conduct to other members, the other house, or its members. Additionally, a Senate rule forbids offensive remarks about any state.

Smoking is not permitted on the floor of either house. On occasion, the Speaker has asked members to leave the floor and return only when properly dressed. Members may not wear hats in their chambers.

Deferral An impoundment of funds for a specific period of time that may not extend beyond the fiscal year in which it is proposed. Under the Impoundment Control Act of 1974, the president must notify Congress that he is deferring the spending or obligation of funds provided by law for a project or activity. Congress can disapprove the deferral by legislation.

The president may defer funds to provide for contingencies when savings have been made through greater operational efficiency or for similar reasons, but not because of opposition to a program, or to reduce federal spending, or for any other policy reason.

Deficit The amount by which the government's outlays exceed its budget receipts for a given fiscal year.

Deficit Neutrality A requirement that certain proposals to increase spending or reduce revenues be offset by at least equivalent reductions in other spending or increases in other revenue sources so that they do not increase the deficit.

Degrees of Amendment Designations that indicate the relationships of amendments to the text of a measure and to each other. In general, an amendment offered directly to the text of a measure is an amendment in the first degree, and an amendment to that amendment is an amendment in the second degree. Both houses normally prohibit amendments in the third degree—that is, an amendment to an amendment to an amendment.

Delegate A nonvoting member of the House of Representatives elected to a two-year term from the District of Columbia, the territory of Guam, the territory of the Virgin Islands, or the territory of American Samoa. By law, delegates may not vote in the full House, but they may participate in debate, offer motions (except to reconsider), and serve and vote on standing and select committees.

Denounce A formal action that condemns a member for misbehavior; considered by some experts to be equivalent to censure. The Senate used it against Sen. Herman Talmadge (D-Ga.) in 1979 and against Sen. David Durenberger (R-Minn.) in 1990.

Deputy President Pro Tempore A position established in 1977 for a sitting senator who is a former president or vice president of the United States. It was originally created for former vice president Hubert H. Humphrey. Ten years later the Senate approved a resolution permitting it to designate any other senator to that position.

Deschler's Precedents Short title for *Deschler's Precedents of the U.S. House of Representatives,* a multivolume compilation and explanation of House precedents and practices since 1936. Begun under the direction of Lewis Deschler, parliamentarian of the House from 1928 to 1974, the first volume was published in 1976.

Dilatory Tactics Procedural actions intended to delay or prevent action by a house or a committee. They include, among others, offering numerous motions, demanding quorum calls and recorded votes at every opportunity, making numerous points of order and parliamentary inquiries, and speaking as long as the applicable rules permit.

Director of Non-Legislative and Financial Services A position created in 1992 to manage most of the financial and general administrative functions of the House of Representatives formerly under the jurisdiction of the clerk, doorkeeper, sergeant at arms, and postmaster of the House.

Discharge a Committee Remove a measure from a committee to which it has been referred in order to make it available for floor consideration. Noncontroversial measures are often discharged by unanimous consent. However, because congressional committees have no obligation to report measures referred to them, each house has procedures to extract controversial measures from recalcitrant committees. In addition, some statutes provide special discharge procedures for specific measures, such as legislative veto resolutions and rescission bills.

Discharge Rule A House rule that provides a lengthy, multistage procedure for removing a measure from a committee. Thirty days after a public bill or resolution has been referred to a committee, any member may file a discharge motion on the measure. A clerk then prepares a discharge petition for members' signatures. If 218 members sign the petition, the motion is placed on the Calendar of Motions to Discharge Committees. After the motion has been on the calendar at least seven days, any member may call it up on the second or fourth Monday of a month. Debate on the discharge motion is limited to twenty minutes, equally divided between proponents and opponents. If the House agrees to the motion, any member who signed the petition may offer a privileged nondebatable motion to consider the discharged measure. Finally, if the House agrees to that motion, it takes up the measure under its general rules.

Discretionary Appropriations Appropriations not mandated by existing law and therefore made available annually in appropriation bills in such amounts as Congress chooses.

Discretionary Recognition The authority of a presiding officer to deny a member's request to speak. In the House of Representatives, the presiding officer has wide discretion in recognition. In the Senate, there is very little discretion.

District Day In the House, one of two days in each month—the second and fourth Mondays—on which business reported and called up by the District of Columbia Committee is privileged for floor consideration.

District Office Representatives maintain one or more offices in their districts for the purpose of assisting constituents. The costs of maintaining these offices are paid from members' allowances. A senator can use the official expense allowance to rent offices in the home state subject to a funding formula based on the state's population, among other factors.

District Work Period The House term for a scheduled congressional recess during which members may visit their districts and conduct constituency business.

Division Vote A vote in which the chair first counts those in favor of a proposition and then those opposed to it, with no record made of how each member votes. In the Senate, the chair may count raised hands or ask senators to stand, whereas the House requires members to stand; hence, often called a standing vote. Committees in both houses ordinarily use a show of hands.

Domestic Discretionary Appropriations Appropriations for domestic programs that are not mandated in entitlement laws and that are therefore made available in such amounts as Congress chooses. Among others, these programs include most government activities in science and space, transportation, medical research, environmental protection, and law enforcement. They are funded in ten of the thirteen annual appropriation bills.

Doorkeeper of the House An officer of the House of Representatives responsible chiefly for enforcing the rules prohibiting unauthorized persons from entering the chamber when the House is in session. Elected by resolution at the beginning of each Congress, the doorkeeper is usually the candidate of the majority party.

E

Early Organization of the House A 1974 House resolution that subsequently became law permits the Democratic Caucus and the Republican Conference to meet in December of even-numbered years to take steps that will facilitate the prompt organization of the House in the upcoming Congress.

Earmark To set aside funds for a specific purpose, use, or recipient. Generally speaking, virtually every appropriation is earmarked, and so are certain revenue sources credited to trust funds. In common usage, however, the term is often applied as an epithet for funds set aside for such purposes as research projects, demonstration projects, parks, laboratories, academic grants, and contracts in particular congressional districts or states or for certain specified universities or other organizations.

Effective Dates Provisions of an act that specify when the entire act or individual provisions in it become effective as law.

Electronic Voting Since 1973 the House has used an electronic voting system to record the yeas and nays and and to conduct recorded votes. Members vote by inserting their voting cards in one of the boxes at several locations in the chamber. They are given at least fifteen minutes to vote. The House also uses the electronic system for quorum calls. The Senate does not have electronic voting.

Enacting Clause The opening language of each bill, beginning "Be it enacted by the Senate and House of Representatives of the United States of America in Congress assembled...."

Engrossed Bill The official copy of a bill or joint resolution as passed by one chamber, including the text as amended by floor action, and certified by the clerk of the House or the secretary of the Senate (as appropriate).

Engrossment and Third Reading The question decided by a house, immediately before it votes on passing a bill or joint resolution, ordering the clerk to engross the measure and to read it by title only. It is invariably ordered without objection.

Enrolled Bill The final official copy of a bill or joint resolution passed in identical form by both houses. An enrolled bill is printed on parchment.

Entitlement Program A federal program under which individuals, businesses, or units of government that meet the requirements or qualifications established by law are entitled to receive certain payments if they seek such payments. Major examples include Social Security, Medicare, Medicaid, unemployment insurance, and military and federal civilian pensions.

Some entitlements are funded by permanent appropriations, others by annual appropriations. In either case, they are a form of backdoor and mandatory spending. Congress cannot control their expenditures by refusing to appropriate the sums necessary to fund them because the government is legally obligated to pay eligible recipients the amounts to which the law entitles them, and recipients can take legal action if the government fails to do so.

Equality of the Houses A component of the Constitution's emphasis on checks and balances under which each house is given essentially equal status in the enactment of legislation and in their relations and negotiations. Although the House of Representatives initiates revenue and appropriation measures, the Senate has the right to amend them. Either house may initiate any other legislation and neither can force the other to agree to, or even act on, its measures. Moreover, each house has a potential veto over the other because measures require agreement by both.

Equally Divided When debate on a matter is limited to a specific length of time, control of the time is usually divided equally between two individuals or two groups. The individuals may be a proponent and opponent, the majority and minority floor managers, or the majority and minority leaders. The groups may be the two political parties, opponents and proponents, or two committees with an equal interest in the matter.

Ethics Rules Several rules or standing orders in each house that mandate certain standards of conduct for members and congressional employees in finance, employment, franking, and other areas.

Ex Officio By virtue of one's office. Under a Senate rule, committee chairmen and ranking minority members may sit ex officio on any of the subcommittees of their committees, but without a vote. Many House committees permit this practice as a matter of custom or committee rule rather than by House rule; some even grant ex officio subcommittee members a vote.

Exclusion The action of a house in refusing to seat a person nominally elected or appointed to it, on the grounds that the individual does not meet the constitutional qualifications for the office or that the election returns are invalid. Usually a house excludes by agreeing to a privileged resolution of exclusion. It only requires a majority vote, even when the individual has been permitted to take the oath of office pending a decision on their right to the seat.

Exclusive Committee (1) Under the rules of the House Democratic Caucus, a standing committee whose Democratic members usually cannot serve on any other standing committee. As of 1993 the Appropriations, Ways and Means, and Rules committees were designated as exclusive committees.

(2) Under the rules of the two party conferences in the Senate, a standing committee

whose members may not simultaneously serve on any other exclusive committee.

Executive Business The Senate term for nominations and treaties the president has submitted to it for approval, under the Senate's "advice and consent" authority.

Executive Calendar The Senate's calendar for committee reports on its executive business, namely treaties and nominations.

Executive Communication A message to Congress from the president or other executive branch official.

Executive Document A document, usually a treaty, sent by the president to the Senate for approval. It is referred to a committee in the same manner as other measures.

Executive Order A unilateral proclamation by the president that has a policy-making or legislative impact. Members of Congress have challenged some executive orders on the grounds that they usurped the authority of the legislative branch. Although the Supreme Court has ruled that a particular order exceeded the president's authority, it has upheld others as falling within the president's general constitutional powers.

Executive Privilege The assertion that presidents have the right to withhold certain information from Congress. Presidents have based their claim on: (1) the constitutional separation of powers; (2) the need for secrecy in military and diplomatic affairs; (3) the need to protect individuals from unfavorable publicity; (4) the need to safeguard the confidential exchange of ideas in the executive branch; and (5) the need to protect individuals who provide confidential advice to the president.

Executive Session (1) A Senate meeting devoted to the consideration of treaties and nominations. Normally, the Senate meets in legislative session, but its rules require that it resolve itself into executive session, by motion or by unanimous consent, to deal with those matters.

(2) A synonym for a committee meeting that is not open to the public.

Expedited Procedures Statutory rules that provide procedures for relatively speedy consideration of certain measures.

Expenditures The amount of government spending other than the net amounts disbursed in the form of loans. Appropriations make monies available for spending or obligation; expenditures are the amounts actually spent. These amounts and appropriated amounts are rarely identical in any fiscal year because some expenditures may come from appropriations made available in previous years, and some appropriations for the current year may be obligated but not actually spent in that year.

Explanatory Statement An explanation of a conference report, endorsed by a majority of the conferees of each house, usually prepared by their staffs.

Expulsion A member's removal from office by a two-thirds vote of his house; the super majority is required by the Constitution. It is the most severe and most rarely used sanction a house can invoke against a member. Although the Constitution provides no explicit grounds for expulsion, the courts have ruled that it may be applied only for misconduct during a member's term of office, not for conduct before the member's election.

Generally, neither house will consider expulsion of a member convicted of a crime until the judicial processes have been exhausted.

Expunging from the *Record* Deletion from the *Congressional Record* of remarks or other materials that violate the rules of a house, such as derogatory statements about another member, profane remarks, or pornographic material.

Extensions of Remarks An appendix to the daily *Congressional Record* that contains miscellaneous extraneous material submitted by members. It often includes members' statements not delivered on the floor, newspaper articles and editorials, praise for a member's constituents, and noteworthy letters received by a member, among other material. Representatives supply the bulk of this material, senators submit very little.

F

Fast-Track Procedures Generally, procedures that circumvent or speed up the usually lengthy legislative process. In the House, these include special procedures in rules reported by the Rules Committee, procedures for dealing with measures on the consent and private calendars, and suspension of the rules. The Senate uses unanimous consent agreements.

Father of the House Unofficial title of the representative with the longest continuous service in the House; also called dean of the House. This member has no official functions but, by custom, administers the oath of office to the Speaker at the beginning of each Congress. No woman has yet reached this rank, so no question has arisen as to what title might be bestowed on such a woman.

Federal Credit Reform Act of 1990 A law that established a system of budgeting for the subsidized cost of federal direct loans and loan guarantees. Under this system, Congress appropriates budget authority or provides indefinite authority equal to the subsidy cost.

Federal Debt The total amount of monies borrowed and not yet repaid by the federal government. Federal debt consists of public debt and agency debt.

Public debt is the portion of the federal debt borrowed by the Treasury or the Federal Financing Bank directly from the public or from another federal fund or account. For example, the Treasury regularly borrows money from the Social Security trust fund. Public debt accounts for about 99 percent of the federal debt.

Agency debt refers to the debt incurred by federal agencies like the Export-Import Bank, but excluding the Treasury and the Federal Financing Bank, which are authorized by law to borrow funds from the public or from another government fund or account.

Federal Regulation of Lobbying Act of 1946 Requires persons attempting to influence the passage or defeat of legislation in Congress to register with the clerk of the House of Representatives or secretary of the Senate and submit quarterly reports on the sources and amounts of money they received and spent for lobbying. The purpose of the law is disclosure, not regulation. The clerk and the secretary compile the information and publish it in the *Congressional Record.*

The Supreme Court has ruled that the law does not apply to (1) persons who spend their own money on lobbying rather than paying someone else to represent them; (2) groups whose principal purpose is something other than lobbying; and (3) persons who do not directly contact members of Congress. Consequently, the law does not effectively provide for disclosure of all lobbying activities.

Field Hearing A committee or subcommittee hearing held outside of Washington, D.C., often in the district or state of a committee member.

Fifteen-Minute Rule A House rule that allows members a minimum of fifteen minutes to cast their votes for the yeas and nays and other recorded votes.

Filibuster The use of obstructive and time-consuming parliamentary tactics by one member or a minority of members to delay, modify, or defeat proposed legislation or rules changes. Filibusters are also sometimes used to delay urgently needed measures in order to force the body to accept other legislation. The Senate's rules permitting unlimited debate and the extraordinary majority it requires to impose cloture make filibustering particularly effective in that chamber. Under the stricter rules of the House, filibusters in that body are short-lived and therefore ineffective and rarely attempted.

Senate filibusters are most likely to succeed when supported by a large minority or when they occur late in a session when time is short and large numbers of must-pass measures are ready for final action. Under those conditions, the threat of a filibuster may force the majority to accept compromises or persuade the leadership to put aside controversial legislation.

Financing Account An account that receives payments from a credit program account established under the terms of the Federal Credit Reform Act of 1990.

Fining a Member In a single instance (1969), the House agreed to a resolution imposing a fine of $25,000 on Rep. Adam Clayton Powell (D-N.Y.) for misbehavior.

Firewall The Budget Enforcement Act of 1990 placed dollar ceilings on three broad categories of federal discretionary spending—defense, international, and domestic—for fiscal years 1991, 1992, and 1993. The act's so-called firewall provisions prevented breaching the spending ceiling of one category by shifting to it funds saved in another category. For example, defense spending could be reduced by a certain amount in order to add those savings to the total available in the domestic category.

First Degree Amendment An amendment offered directly to the text of a measure.

First Reading The required reading to a chamber of a bill or joint resolution by title only after its introduction. The House complies with the first reading by publishing the measure's title in the *Journal* and the *Congressional Record*.

Fiscal Year The federal government's annual accounting period. It begins October 1 and ends on the following September 30. A fiscal year is designated by the calendar year in which it ends and is often referred to as FY. Thus, fiscal year 1992 began October 1, 1991, ended September 30, 1992, and is called FY92.

Five-Minute Rule (1) A House rule that limits debate on an amendment offered in the Committee of the Whole to five minutes for its sponsor and five minutes for an opponent. In practice, the committee routinely permits longer debate by two devices: the offering of pro forma amendments, each debatable for five minutes, and unanimous consent for a member to speak longer than five minutes. Consequently, debate on an amendment sometimes continues for hours or, rarely, for more than a day.

(2) A House rule that limits a committee member to five minutes when questioning a witness at a hearing until each member has had an opportunity to question that witness. Adopted in 1971, the rule prevents any member from monopolizing so much of the time available for questioning so that others are prevented from asking questions.

Floor (1) The ground level of the House or Senate chamber where members sit and the houses conduct their business. When members are attending a meeting of their house, they are said to be "on the floor."

(2) A member recognized by the presiding officer is said to "have the floor" or "hold the floor." When senators finish what they have to say, they often declare, "Mr. President, I yield the floor."

(3) "Floor stage" refers to the stage of the legislative process, usually following the committee stage, when a house takes up a measure.

(4) "Floor action" refers to the procedural actions taken during floor consideration, such as deciding on motions, taking up measures, amending them, and voting.

Floor Amendment An amendment offered on the floor by a member. These amendments are distinguished from committee amendments and certain amendments whose consideration is automatically required by a special rule in the House.

Floor Leader The member elected by each party in each house to be its principal floor spokesman.

Floor Manager A majority party member responsible for guiding a measure through its floor consideration in a house and for devising the political and procedural strategies that might be required to get it passed. The presiding officer gives the floor manager priority recognition to debate, offer amendments, oppose amendments, and make crucial procedural motions.

Frank Informally, a member's legal right to send official mail postage free under his or her signature; often called the franking privilege. Technically, it is the autographic or facsimile signature used on envelopes instead of stamps that permits members and certain congressional officers to send their official mail free of charge. The franking privilege has been authorized by law since the first Congress, except for a few months in 1873. Congress reimburses the U.S. Postal Service for the franked mail it handles.

The frank cannot be used for personal matters or for purposes "unrelated to the official business, activities, and duties" of those who have the privilege. It cannot be used to solicit political support, votes, or financial assistance. Under a House rule adopted in 1993, a representative cannot send any mass mailing outside the congressional district from which he was elected.

Free Vote In congressional jargon, the vote a member casts for a measure or an amendment, even though he thinks it ill-advised or irresponsible, to enhance his popularity with his constituents, but in the expectation that the other chamber will reject it.

Full Funding An appropriation that finances the full estimated cost of a project or activity that will take several years to complete and that requires periodic or intermittent expenditures over that period of time: for example, a construction project or a procurement program. In contrast, incremental funding refers to instances in which Congress provides funds in each fiscal year for only that year's portion of the estimated total cost of the project or activity.

Function *or* Functional Category A broad category of national need and spending of budgetary significance. A category provides an accounting method for allocating and keeping track of budgetary resources and expenditures for that function because it includes all budget accounts related to the function's subject or purpose. A congressional budget resolution lists all the functional categories and the portion of aggregate budget amounts allocated to each.

As of 1992 there were twenty functional categories, each divided into a number of subfunctions. They included such national-need categories as agriculture, administration of justice, commerce and housing credit, energy, income security, transportation, and national defense. Those not assigned to national needs were net interest and undistributed offsetting receipts.

G

Gag Rule A pejorative term for any type of special rule reported by the House Rules Committee that proposes to prohibit amendments to a measure or only permits amendments offered by the reporting committee.

Galleries The balconies overlooking each chamber. From different seating areas in the galleries, the public, news media, staff, and others may observe and listen to the floor proceedings.

General Accounting Office (GAO) A congressional support agency, often referred to as the investigative arm of Congress. It evaluates and audits federal agencies and programs in the United States and abroad on its own initiative or at the request of congressional committees, their chairmen and ranking minority members, or, occasionally, other members. GAO publishes many of its reports and makes them available to interested members and staff.

General Appropriation Bill A term applied to each of the thirteen annual bills that provide funds for most federal agencies and programs and also to the supplemental appropriation bills that contain appropriations for more than one agency or program.

The Constitution does not require annual appropriations, but Congress has funded most agencies and programs annually since the first Congress.

General Debate In the House of Representatives, usually refers to debate at the beginning of proceedings in the Committee of the Whole during which amendments may not be offered. Customarily, the time for general debate is controlled by and divided equally between the majority and minority floor managers of a measure.

Senators seldom use the term. However, the Senate sometimes provides a rough equivalent to general debate under unanimous consent agreements that explicitly set aside time for debate on a bill or on the question of final passage, in addition to time for debate on amendments.

General Leave After the House passes a bill, the floor manager often requests permission or "leave" for all members to insert their statements on it into the *Congressional Record,* usually under a deadline of five legislative days.

General Legislation The Senate term for legislative provisions as distinguished from appropriation provisions. It is roughly synonymous with the term "changing existing law" in the rules of the House.

General Pair A voting pair between two absent members that does not indicate their positions on the question. They may agree or disagree. In the Senate, positions may be inferred when two senators of generally different ideologies announce that they have entered into a general pair.

Gephardt Rule A House rule providing for automatic House passage of a joint resolution increasing the statutory limit on the public debt when the House agrees to a budget resolution that requires such an increase. Rep. Richard A. Gephardt (D-Mo.) was the rule's chief sponsor.

Germane Basically, on the same subject as the matter under consideration. A House rule requires that all amendments be germane. In the Senate, only amendments proposed to general appropriation bills and budget resolutions or under cloture must be germane.

Gerrymandering The manipulation of legislative district boundaries to benefit a particular party, politician, or minority group. The term originated in 1812 when the Massachusetts legislature redrew the lines of state legislative districts to favor the party of Gov. Elbridge Gerry, and some critics said one district looked like a salamander.

Ghost Voting In the House, when someone other than a member casts the member's vote on the floor or records the member as present. In 1980, the House adopted a rule explicitly prohibiting the practice after what the House Manual refers to as "voting anomalies" were discovered in the use of its electronic voting system.

Government-Sponsored Enterprises (GSEs) Enterprises established by the federal government, but privately owned, that engage in credit activities. They are excluded from the federal budget.

Gramm-Rudman-Hollings Act of 1985 Common name for the Balanced Budget and Emergency Deficit Control Act of 1985, which established new budget procedures intended to balance the federal budget by fiscal year 1991—a goal subsequently extended to 1993. To achieve that goal, the act set annual maximum deficit targets and mandated automatic across-the-board spending cuts, called sequesters, by the president to enforce the limits. It also extensively amended the Congressional Budget Act of 1974. The act's chief sponsors were senators Phil Gramm (R-Texas), Warren Rudman (R-N.H.), and Ernest Hollings (D-S.C.).

Grandfather Clause A provision in a measure, law, or rule that exempts an individual, entity, or a defined category of individuals or entities from complying with a new policy or restriction.

Grants-in-Aid Payments by the federal government to state and local governments to help provide for assistance programs or public services.

H

Hearing Committee or subcommittee meetings to receive testimony on proposed legislation during investigations or for oversight purposes. Relatively few bills are important enough to justify formal hearings. Witnesses often include experts, government officials, spokespersons for interested groups, officials of the General Accounting Office, and members of Congress.

Hinds' and Cannon's Precedents of the House of Representatives A monumental, multivolume compilation and detailed explanation of virtually every House precedent from the first Congress (1789-1791) through 1936, arranged by topic. It consists of eleven massive volumes, the last three devoted to the index. The compilers, Asher C. Hinds (R-Maine) and Clarence A. Cannon (D-Mo.), both served the House first as parliamentarians and later as members.

Hold A senator's request that his or her party leaders delay floor consideration of certain legislation or presidential nominations. The majority leader usually honors a hold for a reasonable period of time.

Hold-Harmless Clause In legislation providing a new formula for allocating federal funds, a clause to ensure that recipients of those funds do not receive less in a future year than they did in the current year if the new formula would result in a reduction for them.

Holman Rule A House rule that permits legislation in a general appropriation bill if it is germane to, and clearly retrenches (reduces) amounts in, the bill. Named after its sponsor, Rep. William C. Holman (D-Ind.), it was first adopted in 1876 but has been revised several times since then.

Hopper A box on the clerk's desk in the House chamber into which members deposit bills and resolutions to introduce them.

House Always capitalized when referring to the House of Representatives, but usually not when referring to either the House or the Senate, as in "each house" or "the two houses of Congress."

House Calendar The calendar reserved for all public bills and resolutions that do not raise revenue or directly or indirectly appropriate money or property when they are favorably reported by House committees.

House Manual A commonly used title for the handbook of the rules of the House of Representatives, published in each Congress. Its official title is *Constitution, Jefferson's Manual, and Rules of the House of Representatives*. The text is annotated with pertinent explanations, historical information, and digests of the principal rulings and precedents. Separate sections contain provisions of certain laws applicable to the House and a description of various support services available to members.

House of Representatives The house of Congress in which states are represented roughly in proportion to their populations, but every state is guaranteed at least one representative. By law, the number of voting representatives is fixed at 435. Four delegates and one resident commissioner also serve in the House; they may vote in their committees and in the Committee of the Whole but not in the House sitting as the House.

Although the House and Senate have equal legislative power, the Constitution gives the House sole authority to originate revenue measures. The House also claims the right to originate appropriation measures, a claim the Senate disputes in theory but concedes in practice. The House has the sole power to impeach, and it elects the president when no candidate has received a majority of the electoral votes. It is sometimes referred to as "the lower body."

I

Immunity (1) Members' constitutional protection from lawsuits and arrest in connection with their legislative duties. They may not be tried for libel or slander for anything they say on the floor of a house or in committee. Nor may they be arrested while attending sessions of their houses or when traveling to or from sessions of Congress, except when charged with treason, a felony, or a breach of the peace.

(2) In the case of a witness before a committee, a grant of protection from prosecution based on that person's testimony to the committee. It is used to compel witnesses to testify who would otherwise refuse to do so on the constitutional ground of possible self-incrimination. Under such a grant, none of a witness' testimony may be used against him or her in a court proceeding except in a prosecution for perjury or for giving a false statement to Congress.

Impeachment The first step to remove the president, vice president, or other federal civil officers from office and to disqualify them from any future federal office "of honor, Trust or Profit." An impeachment is a formal charge of treason, bribery, or "other high Crimes and Misdemeanors." The House has the sole power of impeachment and the Senate the sole power of trying the charges and convicting. The House impeaches by a simple majority vote; conviction requires a two-thirds vote of all senators present.

Impoundment An executive branch action or inaction that delays or withholds the expenditure or obligation of budget authority provided by law. The Impoundment Control Act of 1974 classifies impoundments as either deferrals or rescissions, requires the president to notify Congress about all such actions, and gives Congress authority to approve or reject them.

Inflationary Impact Statement A statement of the "inflationary impact on prices and costs in the operation of the national economy" that may result from enactment of a public bill or joint resolution. A House rule requires such statements to appear in its committees' reports on proposed legislation.

Insist A motion by a house to reiterate its previous position during the process of amendments between the houses. A house may insist on its amendment after the other house has disagreed to it, or a house may insist on its previous disagreement to an amendment of the other house.

Inspector General A position created in 1992 to audit the administrative functions of the House of Representatives. Appointed jointly by the Speaker, majority leader, and minority leader, the inspector general reports to them, to the director of non-legislative and financial services, and to the chairman and ranking minority member of the Committee on House Administration.

Instruct Conferees A formal action by a house urging its conferees to uphold a particular position on a measure in conference. The instruction may be to insist on certain provisions in the measure as passed by that house or to accept a provision in the version passed by the other house. Conferees are not bound by such instruction, however.

International Discretionary Appropriations Appropriations not mandated in law, and therefore made available in appropriation bills in such amounts as Congress chooses, for foreign economic and military aid, the State Department, the U.S. Information Agency, and international financial programs such as the U.S. Export-Import Bank.

Investigative Power The authority of Congress and its committees to pursue investigations, upheld by the Supreme Court but limited to matters "related to, and in furtherance of, a legitimate task of the Congress." Standing committees in both houses are permanently authorized to investigate matters within their jurisdictions. Major investigations are sometimes conducted by temporary select, special, or joint committees established by resolutions for that purpose.

Investigative Staff Committee staff authorized by annual or biennial resolutions rather than by rule or law; also called temporary staff. They are paid from the contingent fund in their respective houses. The term is somewhat misleading; many staff authorized by resolutions do not perform investigative functions and most continue to serve for indefinite and often extended periods. Since 1981, all Senate committee staff have been authorized by resolutions.

Iron Triangle A term sometimes used by scholars and journalists when referring to the alliances often found among a committee, the officials of an agency under its jurisdiction, and lobbyists interested in programs administered by the agency.

Item Veto A suggested presidential authority to veto a portion of a measure rather than all of it as is now required; sometimes called a line-item veto.

J

Jefferson's Manual Short title of *Jefferson's Manual of Parliamentary Practice,* prepared by Thomas Jefferson for his own guidance when he was president of the Senate from 1797 to 1801. Although it reflects English parliamentary practice in his day, many procedures in both houses of Congress are still rooted in its basic precepts.

Johnson Rule A policy instituted in 1953 under which all Democratic senators are assigned to one major committee before any Democrat is assigned to two. The Johnson Rule is named after its author, Sen. Lyndon B. Johnson (D-Texas), then the Senate's Democratic leader. Senate Republicans adopted a similar policy soon thereafter.

Joint Committee A committee composed of members selected from each house. The functions of most joint committees involve investigation, research, or oversight of agencies closely related to Congress. Permanent joint committees, created by statute, are sometimes called standing joint committees.

Joint Referral Another term for a multiple referral: the referral of a measure to two or more committees simultaneously.

Joint Resolution A legislative measure that Congress uses for purposes other than general legislation. Like a bill, it has the force of law when passed by both houses and either approved by the president or passed over the president's veto. Unlike a bill, a joint resolution enacted into law is not called an act; it retains its original title.

Most often, joint resolutions deal with such relatively limited matters as the correction of errors in existing law, continuing appropriations, a single appropriation, or the establishment of permanent joint committees. Unlike bills, however, joint resolutions also are used to propose constitutional amendments; these do not require the president's signature and become effective only when ratified by three-fourths of the states.

The House designates joint resolutions as H. J. Res., the Senate as S. J. Res. Each house numbers its joint resolutions consecutively in the order of introduction during a two-year Congress.

Joint Rules Rules governing the procedure of the two houses in matters requiring their concurrent action. Congress adopted a number of joint rules in its early years, but abrogated them in 1876. In the 91st Congress (1969-1971), however, a law specifying that the counting of electoral votes for president and vice president should be conducted in joint session was made a joint rule.

Joint Session Informally, any combined meeting of the Senate and the House. Technically, a joint session is a combined meeting to count the electoral votes for president and vice president or to hear a presidential address, such as the State of the Union message; any other formal combined gathering of both houses is called a joint meeting. Joint sessions are held in the House chamber because of its larger seating capacity.

Joint Sponsorship Two or more members sponsoring the same measure.

Journal The official record of House or Senate actions, including every motion offered, every vote cast, amendments agreed to, quorum calls, and so forth. Unlike the *Congressional Record*, it does not provide reports of speeches, debates, statements, and the like. The Constitution requires each house to maintain a *Journal* and to publish it periodically. The House keeps a single *Journal* but the Senate keeps four: one for its legislative sessions; a second, titled *Executive Proceedings in the Senate*, for its executive business sessions; a third for confidential legislative proceedings; and the fourth for proceedings when it sits as a court of impeachment.

Junior Senator The senator who has served for a shorter continuous period in the Senate than the other senator from the same state.

Junket A member's trip at government expense, especially abroad, ostensibly on official business but, it is often alleged, for pleasure.

K

Killer Amendment An amendment that, if agreed to, might lead to the defeat of the measure it amends, either in the house in which the amendment is offered or at some later stage of the legislative process.

King of the Mountain (*or* Hill) Rule A special rule from the House Rules Committee that permits votes on a series of amendments, especially complete substitutes for a measure, in a specified order, but directs that the last amendment agreed to shall be the winning one.

This kind of rule permits the House to vote directly on a variety of alternatives to a measure, but it also gives the last amendment a potential advantage over the others.

L

Lame Duck Jargon for a member who has not been reelected, or did not seek reelection, and is serving the balance of his or her term.

Lame Duck Session A session of a Congress held after the election for the succeeding Congress, so-called after the lame duck members still serving.

Last Train Out Jargon for the last must-pass bill of a session of Congress.

Law An act of Congress that has been signed by the president or passed over the president's veto.

Law Revision Counsel A statutory position in the House of Representatives. The counsel's chief function is to develop a codification of U.S. laws.

Lay on the Table A motion to dispose of a pending proposition immediately, finally, and adversely; that is, to kill it without a direct vote on its substance. Informally referred to as a motion to table, it is not debatable and is adopted by majority vote or without objection. It is a highly privileged motion, taking precedence over all others except the motion to adjourn in the House and all but three additional motions in the Senate. It can kill a bill, resolution, amendment, another motion, a point of order, an appeal, or virtually any other matter.

Layover Rules Rules that require a specified period of time to elapse before action may be taken on certain measures, motions, or other matters.

Leadership Usually, a reference to the majority and minority leaders of the Senate or to the Speaker and minority leader of the House. The term sometimes includes the majority leader in the House and the majority and minority whips in each house, and, at other times, other party officials as well.

Leave of Absence A formal grant of permission for a member to be absent during the proceedings of the member's house.

A Senate rule prohibits senators from absenting themselves "from the service of the Senate without leave." In practice, requests for leave are routinely granted.

A House rule requires every member to be "present within the Hall of the House during its sittings, unless excused or necessarily prevented." In practice, two types of absence are permitted: (1) temporary ones granted during the call of the roll; and (2) leaves of absence lasting at least one day, usually granted by unanimous consent at the end of a day's legislative program.

Leave to Sit Permission for a committee to meet during certain proceedings of its house when most committees are forbidden to meet.

Legislation (1) A synonym for legislative measures: bills and joint resolutions.

(2) Provisions in such measures or in substantive amendments offered to them.

(3) In some contexts, provisions that change existing substantive or authorizing law, rather than provisions that make appropriations.

Legislation on an Appropriation Bill A common reference to provisions changing existing law that appear in, or are offered as amendments to, a general appropriation bill. A House rule prohibits the inclusion of such provisions in general appropriation bills unless they retrench expenditures. An analogous Senate rule permits points of order against amendments to a general appropriation bill that propose "general legislation." The intent of both rules is to enforce the separation between substantive legislation and appropriations legislation.

Legislative Assistant (LA) A member's staff person responsible for monitoring and preparing legislation on particular subjects and for advising the member on them; commonly referred to as an LA.

Legislative Authority (1) A synonym for an authorization of appropriations.

(2) A committee's authority to report legislation to its chamber.

Legislative Calendar Informal title for the Senate's calendar of general orders on which legislative measures are placed.

Legislative Committee (1) A committee authorized to report legislation to its parent body, as distinguished from an investigative, study, or party committee.

(2) A term sometimes applied to a committee that reports authorizing legislation rather than appropriation measures.

Legislative Counsel's Office In each house, a staff of attorneys who provide nonpartisan, expert assistance in drafting bills, resolutions, and amendments, primarily to committees.

The House Legislative Counsel is appointed by the Speaker, the Senate's by the president pro tempore. In turn, they appoint the other attorneys in their respective offices.

Legislative Day The "day" that begins when a house meets after an adjournment and ends when it next adjourns. Because the House of Representatives normally adjourns at the end of a daily session, its legislative and calendar days usually coincide. The Senate, however, frequently recesses at the end of a daily session, and its legislative day may extend over several calendar days, weeks, or months.

Among other uses, this technicality permits the Senate to save time by circumventing its morning hour, a procedure required at the beginning of every legislative day. On occasion, the House or Senate has adjourned in the middle of a calendar day and immediately reconvened in a new legislative "day" to circumvent its one-day layover rules.

Legislative History (1) A chronological list of actions taken on a measure during its progress through the legislative process.

(2) The official documents relating to a measure, the entries in the *Journals* of the two houses on that measure, and the *Congressional Record* text of its consideration in both houses. The documents include all committee reports and the conference report and joint explanatory statement, if any.

Courts and affected federal agencies study a measure's legislative history for congressional intent about its purpose and interpretation. They pay particular attention to statements in standing and conference committee reports and during floor debates in both houses about the meaning and intended interpretation of individual provisions in the measure and in amendments to it.

Legislative Process (1) Narrowly, the stages in the enactment of a law from introduction to final disposition. An introduced measure that becomes law typically travels through reference to committee; committee and subcommittee consideration; report to the chamber; floor consideration; amendment; passage; engrossment; messaging to the other house; similar steps in that house including floor amendment of the measure; return of the measure to the first house; consideration of amendments between the houses or a conference to resolve their differences; approval of the conference report by both houses; enrollment; approval by the president or override of the president's veto; and deposit with the archivist of the United States.

(2) Broadly, the political, lobbying, and other factors that affect or influence the process of enacting laws.

Legislative Service Organizations (LSOs) The House title for more than 100 unofficial groups of representatives formed to focus attention or advocate action on one or more national policies or on issues important to their constituencies. Smaller, newer groups are formally called congressional member organizations. Both groups are sometimes called informal caucuses.

Most groups consist entirely of House members, a few are for senators only, and a number have bicameral memberships. Many have paid staff, office space, dues-paying members, bylaws, and elected officers.

LSOs are either partisan and ideological, such as the Democratic Study Group and the House Republican Study Committee, or they are nonpartisan and focus on the interests of certain populations or industries.

Legislative Session A Senate meeting to consider legislative business rather than treaties and nominations. The latter are considered in executive session. Under Senate rules, the chamber meets in legislative session unless it agrees by unanimous consent or by motion to go into executive session. It requires the same procedure to return to legislative session.

Legislative Veto A procedure, declared unconstitutional in 1983, that allowed Congress or one of its houses to nullify certain actions of the president, executive branch agencies, or independent agencies. Sometimes called congressional vetoes or congressional disapprovals. Concurrent resolutions were required for vetoes involving both houses, simple resolutions for action by one house. These procedures reversed the usual roles of the two branches, permitting the executive, in effect, to make law subject to a veto by the legislature.

Following the Supreme Court's 1983 decision, Congress amended several legislative veto statutes to require enactment of joint resolutions, which are subject to presidential veto, for nullifying executive branch actions.

Limitation on a General Appropriation Bill Language that prohibits expenditures for part of an authorized purpose from funds provided in a general appropriation bill. Precedents require that the language be phrased in the negative: that none of the funds provided in a paragraph or the act shall be used for a specified activity.

Limitations in general appropriation bills are permitted on the grounds that Congress can refuse to fund authorized programs and, therefore, can refuse to fund any part of them as long as the prohibition does not change existing law. House precedents have established that a limitation does not change existing law if it does not impose additional duties or burdens on executive branch officials, interfere with their discretionary authority, or require them to make judgments or determinations not required by existing law.

Line Item Generally, an amount in an appropriation measure. It can refer to a single appropriation account or to separate amounts within the account.

Liquidating Appropriation An appropriation to pay obligations incurred under contract authority.

Live Pair A voluntary and informal agreement between two members on opposite sides of an issue under which the member who is present for a recorded vote withholds or withdraws his or her vote because the other member is absent. Usually, the member in attendance announces that he or she has a live pair, states how each would have voted, and votes "present."

Live Quorum In the Senate, a quorum call to which senators are expected to respond by going to the floor. Usually, senators suggest the absence of a quorum not to force a quorum to appear, but merely to provide a pause in the proceedings during which senators can engage in private discussions or wait for a senator to come to the floor.

Loan Guarantee A statutory commitment by the federal government to pay part or all of a loan's principal and interest to a lender or the holder of a security in case the borrower defaults.

Lobby To try to persuade members of Congress to propose, pass, modify, or defeat proposed legislation or to change or repeal existing laws. A lobbyist attempts to promote his or her own preferences or those of a group, organization, or industry. Originally the term referred to persons frequenting the lobbies or corridors of legislative chambers in order to speak to lawmakers.

The right to lobby stems from the First Amendment to the Constitution, which bans laws that abridge the right of the people "to petition the government for a redress of grievances." A federal law tries to force disclosure of lobbying activities by requiring persons who receive and spend money for that purpose to register with (and submit quarterly statements to) the clerk of the House or secretary of the Senate.

In a general sense, lobbying includes not only direct contact with members but also indirect attempts to influence them, such as writing to them or persuading others to write or visit them, attempting to mold public opinion toward a desired legislative goal by various means, and contributing or arranging for contributions to members' election campaigns. The Supreme Court has taken a much narrower view of lobbying in its interpretation of federal law.

Locality Rule A custom, rather than a rule, that a member of the House of Representatives should reside in the district he or she represents.

Logrolling Jargon for a legislative tactic or bargaining strategy in which members try to build support for their legislation by promising to support legislation desired by other members or by accepting amendments they hope will induce their colleagues to vote for their bill.

Lower Body A common reference to the House of Representatives, but one that House members consider pejorative.

M

Mace The symbol of the office of the House sergeant at arms. Under the direction of the Speaker, the sergeant at arms is responsible for preserving order on the House floor by holding up the mace in front of an unruly member, or by carrying the mace up and down the aisles to quell boisterous behavior.

When the House is in session, the mace sits on a pedestal at the Speaker's right; when the House is in Committee of the Whole, it is moved to a lower pedestal.

The mace is 46 inches high and consists of 13 ebony rods bound in silver and topped by a silver globe with a silver eagle, wings outstretched, perched on it.

Main Question A measure, motion, or proposal under consideration, as distinguished from the amendments to it. In the House, members may speak once on the main question and once on each amendment.

Major Committees The rules of the House Democratic Caucus apply this designation to certain committees and state that no Democratic representative may serve on more than one of them. As of 1993, the major committees were Agriculture; Armed Services; Banking, Finance, and Urban Affairs; Education and Labor; Foreign Affairs; Energy and Commerce; Judiciary; and Public Works and Transportation.

Majority Leader The majority party's chief floor spokesman, elected by that party's caucus—sometimes called floor leader.

In the Senate, the majority leader also develops the party's political and procedural strategy, usually in collaboration with other party officials and committee chairmen. He negotiates the Senate's agenda and committee ratios with the minority leader and usually calls up measures for floor action.

In the House, the majority leader is the Speaker's deputy and heir apparent. He helps plan the floor agenda and the party's legislative strategy and often speaks for the party leadership in debate.

Majority Vote Although not explicitly stated in the rules of either house, both houses decide questions by a majority vote of the members voting except when the Constitution or the rules require otherwise.

Managers (1) The official title of members appointed to a conference committee, commonly called conferees. The ranking majority and minority managers for each house also manage floor consideration of the committee's conference report.

(2) The members who manage the initial floor consideration of a measure.

Mandatory Appropriations Amounts that Congress must appropriate annually because it has no discretion over them unless it first amends existing substantive law.

Markup A meeting or series of meetings by a committee or subcommittee during which members "mark up" a measure by offering, debating, and voting on amendments to it.

Means-Tested Programs Programs that provide benefits or services to low-income individuals who meet a test of need. Most are entitlement programs, such as Medicaid, food stamps, and Supplementary Security Income.

Meeting Hour The hour each house establishes for convening its daily meetings. Each does so by agreeing to a standing order: the Senate at the beginning of each Congress and the House at the beginning of each session of Congress.

Although the Senate traditionally fixes noon as its convening hour, the majority leader often alters the time from day to day—by unanimous consent—to cope with the ebb and flow of the chamber's workload.

In 1993, the House standing order fixed its meeting hour at noon on Mondays and Tuesdays, 2 p.m. on Wednesdays, and 11 a.m. on all other days, until May 15. For the remainder of the session, the daily meeting time was set at noon on Mondays and Tuesdays and 10 a.m. on all other days.

Member (1) Generic term for one who serves in the House of Representatives or Senate.

(2) One who serves on a committee.

Members' Allowances Official expenses that are paid for or for which members are reimbursed by their houses. Among these are the costs of office space in congressional buildings and in their home states or districts; office equipment and supplies; postage-free mailings (the franking privilege); a set number of trips to and from home states or districts, as well as travel elsewhere on official business; telephone and other telecommunications services; and staff salaries.

All allowances are authorized by law, but each house determines for itself the details and regulations governing many of them. Some allowances are subject to dollar limits, others are not. The two houses sometimes differ on these and other conditions.

Message An official communication between the houses or from the president to one or both houses. Messages between the houses are used principally to transmit a measure a house has passed or a measure with amendments between the houses. Presidential messages might contain legislative suggestions, a veto, or other information.

Method of Equal Proportions The mathematical formula used since 1950 to determine how the 435 seats in the House of Representatives should be distributed among the 50 states in the apportionment following each decennial census. It minimizes as much as possible the proportional difference between the average district population in any two states.

Because the Constitution guarantees each state at least one representative, fifty seats are automatically apportioned. The formula calculates priority numbers for each state, assigns the first of the 385 remaining seats to the state with the highest priority number, the second to the state with the next highest number, and so on until all seats are distributed.

Mid-Session Budget Review A report to Congress that is prepared by the Office of Management and Budget updating the president's budget estimates and economic forecast. The president is required to submit it no later than July 15 each year.

Midterm Election The general election for members of Congress that occurs in November of the second year in a presidential term.

Minority Leader The minority party's leader and chief floor spokesman, elected by the party caucus; sometimes called minority floor leader. With the assistance of other party officials and the ranking minority members of committees, the minority leader devises the party's political and procedural strategy.

Minority Staff The staff who assist the minority party members of a committee. The Senate's rules on minority staff are more generous than those of the House. Its regulation declares that a committee's staff should reflect the relative number of the committee's majority and minority members and guarantees the minority at least one-third of the funds available for staff.

In the House, a majority of a standing committee's minority members are authorized to select six of its eighteen professional staff and four of its twelve clerical permanent staff, but these selections are subject to approval by the full committee in each individual case. The rule also permits the ranking minority member of a standing subcommittee to appoint one staff member to serve at his or her pleasure. However, House rules do not guarantee minority members control over the hiring of any investigative staff.

Modified Rule A special rule from the House Rules Committee that permits only certain amendments to be offered to a measure during its floor consideration or that bans certain specified amendments or amendments on certain subjects.

Morning Business In the Senate, routine business transacted at the beginning of the morning hour at the demand of any senator.

Morning Hour A two-hour period at the beginning of a new legislative day during which the Senate is supposed to conduct routine business, call the calendar on Mondays, and deal with other matters described in a Senate rule. In practice, it often does not occur because the Senate frequently recesses, rather than adjourns, at the end of a daily session and therefore the rule does not apply when it next meets.

Motion A formal proposal for a procedural action, such as to consider, to amend, to lay on the table, to reconsider, to recess, or to adjourn. It has been estimated that at least eighty-five motions are possible under various circumstances in the House, somewhat fewer in the Senate.

Multiple and Sequential Referrals The practice of referring a measure simultaneously to two or more committees for concurrent consideration (multiple or joint referral), or successively to several committees in sequence (sequential referral). A measure may also be divided into several parts, each referred to a different committee or to several committees sequentially (split referral). In theory, this gives all committees that have jurisdiction over parts of a measure the opportunity to report on them.

Multiyear Appropriation An appropriation that remains available for spending or obligation for more than one fiscal year.

Multiyear Authorization (1) Legislation that authorizes the existence or continuation of an agency, program, or activity for more than one fiscal year.

(2) Legislation that authorizes appropriations for an agency, program, or activity for more than one fiscal year.

Must-Pass Bill Congressional jargon for a bill whose passage is critically important, often because it is needed to continue the operations of the federal government, to pay for its obligations, or to protect its credit. Chief among must-pass bills are the regular annual appropriation bills, continuing resolutions, and bills to raise the federal debt ceiling. Because the president is usually reluctant to veto such measures, members often try to attach riders to them that the president might reject if sent to him separately.

N

Nomination A proposed presidential appointment to a federal office submitted to the Senate for confirmation. Approval is by majority vote.

The Constitution explicitly requires confirmation for ambassadors, consuls, "public Ministers" (department heads), and Supreme Court justices. By law, other federal judges, all military promotions of officers, and many high-level civilian officials must be confirmed. Nominations lapse if the Senate does not approve them before sine die adjournment or before it adjourns or recesses for more than thirty days. If the president wants a decision on these nominations, they must be resubmitted during the next session.

In any year, the Senate processes almost 40,000 nominations, most of them for military positions and the vast bulk with little debate or objection.

Nondebatable Motions Motions that must be put to an immediate vote without discussion. Both houses prohibit debate on the motions to adjourn, recess, and lay on the table. Other major nondebatable motions in the Senate include those to consider conference reports, to consider measures during the morning hour, and to close the doors. Other nondebatable House motions include a call of the House, to order the previous question, to resolve into the Committee of the Whole, that the Committee of the Whole rise and report, to close general debate, and to close debate on amendments in the Committee of the Whole.

Nonlegislative Period The Senate term for a scheduled congressional recess during which senators can visit their states and meet with constituents.

Nonmajor Committees The rules of the House Democratic Caucus apply this designation to ten committees and state that no Democratic representative can serve on more than two of them. A member who serves on a major committee is limited to one nonmajor committee assignment. As of 1993, the following committees were considered nonmajor: Budget; District of Columbia; Government Operations; House Administration; Merchant Marine and Fisheries; Natural Resources; Post Office and Civil

Service; Science, Space, and Technology; Small Business; and Veterans' Affairs.

O

Oath of Office Upon taking office, members of Congress must swear or affirm that they will "support and defend the Constitution ... against all enemies, foreign and domestic," that they will "bear true faith and allegiance" to the Constitution, that they take the obligation "freely, without any mental reservation or purpose of evasion," and that they will "well and faithfully discharge the duties" of their office. The oath is required by the Constitution; the wording is prescribed by a statute.

All House members must take the oath at the beginning of each new Congress. Usually, the member with the longest continuous service in the House swears in the Speaker, who then swears in the other members. The president of the Senate or a surrogate administers the oath to newly elected senators.

Oaths to Witnesses A statute empowers House and Senate chairmen and members of select or standing committees to administer oaths to witnesses. It also gives the same power to the Speaker and to chairmen of the Committee of the Whole in the House, an authority not exercised in recent times.

Obligated Balance The amount of an appropriation that has been obligated but not spent. Usually this balance is carried forward to succeeding fiscal years until the obligations are paid.

Obligation A binding agreement by a government agency to pay for goods, products, services, studies, and the like, either immediately or in the future. When an agency enters into such an agreement, it incurs an obligation. As the agency makes the required payments, it liquidates the obligation.

Appropriation laws usually make funds available for obligation for one or more fiscal years but do not require agencies to spend their funds during those specific years. The actual outlays can occur years after the appropriation is obligated.

Off-Budget Entities Specific federal entities whose budget authority, outlays, and receipts are excluded by law from the calculation of budget totals, although they are part of government spending and income. As of early 1993, these included the Social Security trust funds (Federal Old-Age and Survivors Insurance Fund and the Federal Disability Insurance Trust Fund) and the Postal Service. Government-sponsored enterprises are also excluded from the budget.

Office of Technology Assessment (OTA) A support agency that assists Congress by producing or contracting for expert studies on the beneficial and adverse affects of the application of current and prospective technologies.

Officers of Congress The Constitution refers to the Speaker of the House and the president of the Senate as officers and declares that each house "shall chuse" its "other Officers," but does not name them or indicate how they should be selected. A House rule refers to its clerk, sergeant at arms, doorkeeper, and chaplain as officers.

Officers are not named in the Senate's rules, but *Riddick's Senate Procedure* lists the president pro tempore, secretary of the Senate, sergeant at arms, chaplain, and the secretaries for the majority and minority parties as officers. A few appointed officials are sometimes referred to as officers, including the parliamentarians and the legislative counsels.

Official Objectors House members who screen measures on the consent calendar or private calendar. They object to those measures that violate certain generally accepted criteria and also to other measures at the request of a party colleague.

Offsetting Receipts Funds collected by the federal government that are not counted as revenue. Instead, they are deducted from outlays and are called negative outlays.

Omnibus Bill A measure that combines the provisions of several disparate subjects into a single and often lengthy bill. Examples include reconciliation bills, continuing resolutions that contain all or most of the thirteen general appropriation bills, and omnibus claims bills that combine several private bills into one measure.

One-Minute Speeches Addresses by House members on any subject but limited to one minute each, usually permitted at the beginning of a daily session after the chaplain's prayer and approval of the *Journal.* They are a customary practice, not a right granted by rule.

One-Speech Rule (1) A House rule limits members to one speech on any question unless the House permits otherwise. A member may speak once on a measure, once on each amendment to it, and once on any debatable motion because the limitation applies to each question.

(2) A Senate rule limits senators to one speech of no more than five minutes on a measure and five minutes on each amendment to it during a call of the calendar.

One-Year Appropriation An appropriation made available for spending or obligation during a single year, usually the fiscal year specified in the enacting clause of the appropriation act. Any portion of an agency's one-year appropriation that it does not spend or obligate during that fiscal year is said to lapse, and the agency loses it.

Open Hearing A committee hearing that the press and public can attend.

Open Rule A special rule from the House Rules Committee that permits members to offer as many floor amendments as they wish as long as the amendments are germane and do not violate other House rules.

Open to Amendment at Any Point A procedural situation in which members may offer amendments to any part of a pending measure in no particular order. This contrasts with situations in which a measure is considered for amendment section by section, or title by title, and only amendments to the pending section or title are permitted. In the Senate, all measures are open to amendment at any point.

Order (1) As a noun, a continuing or temporary regulation or directive not incorporated into a chamber's standing rules. Continuing orders are called standing orders. Temporary ones are sometimes called special orders. Both types are created either by unanimous consent or by adopting a resolution.

(2) Compliance with the rules and practices of appropriate parliamentary behavior during meetings of a house or a committee.

(3) Precedence of certain actions, such as the order of business or the voting order on amendments.

(4) As a verb, the term used for approval of certain actions, such as to order the yeas and nays, the previous question, or engrossment and third reading of a measure.

Order of Business (House) The sequence of events during the meeting of the House on a new legislative day prescribed by a House rule; also called the general order of business. The sequence consists of (1) the chaplain's prayer; (2) approval of the *Journal*; (3) correction of the reference of public bills; (4) disposal of business on the Speaker's table; (5) unfinished business; (6) the morning hour call of committees and consideration of their bills (largely obsolete); (7) motions to go into Committee of the Whole; and (8) orders of the day (also obsolete).

In practice, on days specified in the rules, the items of business that follow approval of the *Journal* are supplanted in part by the special order of business (for example, the consent, discharge, or private calendars) and on any day by other privileged business (for example, general appropriation bills and special rules) or measures made in order by special rules.

Order of Business (Senate) The sequence of events at the beginning of a new legislative day prescribed by Senate rules. The sequence consists of (1) the chaplain's prayer; (2) *Journal* reading and correction; (3) morning business in the morning hour; (4) call of the calendar during the morning hour; and (5) unfinished business.

Ordered Reported A committee's formal action of agreeing to report a measure to its house for floor consideration.

Organization of Congress The actions the two houses take at the beginning of a Congress that are necessary to their operations. These include swearing in newly elected members, notifying the president that a quorum of each house is present, making committee assignments, and fixing the hour for daily meetings.

Original Jurisdiction The authority of certain committees to originate a measure and report it to the chamber. For example, general appropriation bills reported by the House Appropriations Committee are original bills, and special rules reported by the House Rules Committee are original resolutions.

Origination Clause Clause 1 of Article I, Section 7 of the Constitution, which grants the House the sole prerogative to originate revenue legislation.

Other Body A commonly used reference to a house by a member of the other house. Congressional comity discourages members from directly naming the other house during debate.

Outlays Amounts of government spending. They consist of payments, usually by check or in cash, to liquidate obligations incurred in prior fiscal years as well as in the current year, including the net lending of funds under budget authority. In federal budget accounting, net outlays are calculated by subtracting the amounts of refunds and various kinds of reimbursements to the government from actual spending.

Override a Veto Congressional enactment of a measure over the president's veto. A veto override requires a recorded two-thirds vote of those voting in each house, a quorum being present. Because the president must return the vetoed measure to its house of origin, that house votes first, but neither house is required to attempt an override, whether immediately or at all. If an override attempt fails in the house of origin, the veto stands and the measure dies.

Oversight Congressional review of the way in which federal agencies implement laws to ensure that they are carrying out the intent of Congress and to inquire into the efficiency of the implementation and the effectiveness of the law. The Legislative Reorganization Act of 1946 defined oversight as the function of exercising continuous watchfulness over the execution of the laws by the executive branch.

The rules of both houses assign this responsibility to their standing committees and direct them to determine, on the basis of their reviews, whether laws within their respective jurisdictions should be changed or if additional laws are necessary. The function is also sometimes called legislative review.

P

Page and Line Identification The system used to identify the location of text in bills and resolutions. The lines on each page of a measure, as well as the pages, are sequentially numbered.

Pairing A procedure that permits two or three members to enter into voluntary arrangements that offset their votes so that one or more of the members can be absent without changing the result. The names of paired members and their positions on the vote (except on general pairs) appear in the *Congressional Record.* Members can be paired on one vote or on a series of votes.

Pairs take three forms: (1) In a live pair, a member on one side who is present withholds his vote when his pair partner on the other side is absent. On a two-thirds vote, two members in favor withhold their votes to offset the absence of one opponent, or one opponent withholds his vote when two favoring the question are absent.

(2) In a specific pair, sometimes called a special or dead pair, both members (or all three) are absent, and the *Record* identifies how they would have voted.

(3) In a general pair, absent members are listed as paired with no indication how either might have voted. Therefore it no longer has any practical purpose.

In the House, party pair clerks help arrange these informal agreements. Leadership staff handle them in the Senate. Pairs are not enforceable because they are informal arrangements.

Pairs are not counted in tabulating the final results of recorded votes so the outcomes are not affected by specific and general pairs; if the members had been present, their votes would have added equally to both sides. But a live pair subtracts a vote that might otherwise have been counted, and several of them, or even one, may affect the outcome of a close vote.

Pairing is one of the many practices Congress copied from the British House of Commons, where it had been used at least as early as 1743. When a pair resulted in the defeat of a resolution in the House in 1840, John Quincy Adams denounced it as a violation of the Constitution and unsuccessfully tried to outlaw the practice. The House did not permit pairing in the Committee of the Whole until 1975.

(The) Papers Certain documents that are passed back and forth between the houses as they attempt to resolve their differences on a measure.

Parliamentarian The official advisor to the presiding officer in each house on questions of procedure. The parliamentarian and his assistants also answer procedural questions from members and congressional staff, refer measures to committees on behalf of the presiding officer, and maintain compilations of the precedents.

Either a parliamentarian or an assistant is always present and near the podium during sessions of each house.

The Speaker appoints the House parliamentarian. Nominally, the secretary of the Senate appoints its parliamentarian, but always with the approval of the majority leader.

Parliamentary Inquiry A member's question, posed to the presiding officer, about a pending procedural situation. Although not required to answer such questions, the chair usually does if they are proper inquiries and properly made.

Parliamentary Law The formal rules governing the methods of procedure, discussion, and debate in deliberative bodies and organized assemblies. The House of Representatives follows general parliamentary law at the beginning of a new Congress before it adopts its own rules. As understood in the House, this law is founded in *Jefferson's Manual* as modified by the practice of U.S. legislative assemblies, especially the House itself.

Party Caucus Generic term for each party's official organization in each house. Only House Democrats officially call their organization a caucus. House and Senate Republicans and Senate Democrats call their organizations conferences.

The party caucuses elect their leaders, approve committee assignments and chairmanships (or ranking minority members, if the party is in the minority), establish party committees and study groups, and discuss party and legislative policies. On rare occasions, they have stripped members of committee seniority or expelled them from the caucus for party disloyalty. In the past, the House and Senate Democratic caucuses had so-called binding rules that required their members to support a party position adopted by a super majority of the caucus on threat of expulsion.

Caucus rules of both parties in both houses place certain limitations on the number of chairmanships or ranking minority positions a member may hold and on members' assignments to certain types of committees. House Democratic Caucus rules require certain procedures for the election of subcommittee chairmen and members and limit the number of such chairmanships any member can hold.

Some House Democratic Caucus rules have a direct impact on House floor and committee procedures. Under one rule, if at least fifty Democrats oppose a special rule that prohibits a germane amendment, Democratic members of the Rules Committee may not support that rule unless the caucus decides otherwise. Another rule limits the kinds of measures the Speaker may schedule for suspension of the rules. Still another rule directs committee chairmen to permit subcommittee chairmen to handle floor consideration of legislation from their respective subcommittees.

Democratic Caucus rules also require a minimum of three Democrats for each two Republican members on standing committees, limit the number of subcommittees on those committees, and prescribe the maximum sizes for subcommittees. Finally, a caucus rule directs that the ratio of Democratic to Republican conference managers be at least as favorable as their ratio on the committee from which they are selected.

Party Tables Tables in the House chamber on the Democratic and Republican sides of the aisle that are reserved for the use of their respective party members. Those who do not wish to speak from the well of the House use the microphones attached to their party tables. Party tables are also called committee tables because the committee floor managers of a measure sit at them during House consideration of the measure.

Passed The term applied to bills and joint resolutions that have been approved by a house.

Pastore Rule Familiar title of a Senate rule requiring that "all debate shall be germane and confined to the specific question then pending" during the first three hours of a day. Germane debate in the Senate is not required under any other circumstances. The rule's author was Sen. John O. Pastore (D-R.I.).

Pay-As-You-Go (PAYGO) A requirement of the Budget Enforcement Act of 1990, effective for fiscal years 1991-1995, that congressional action on revenue legislation and legislation on entitlement or other mandatory programs should not add to the budget deficit. Increased spending for such programs resulting from new legislation and revenue losses from legislation reducing taxes or fees are supposed to be offset by legislated spending reductions in other programs subject to PAYGO or by legislated increases in other taxes.

If Congress fails to enact the appropriate offsets, the act requires presidential sequestration of sufficient offsetting amounts in specific direct spending accounts.

Pending Amendment(s) In the singular, the amendment on which the next vote will occur. In the plural, all amendments that have been offered but not yet voted on, withdrawn, or temporarily laid aside. The number of pending amendments to a measure usually does not exceed four or five, but Senate practices permit as many as seven, and nine are possible in the House.

Pending Business A measure or matter that a house is considering. In both houses, certain rules apply only to pending business.

Perfecting Amendment An amendment other than a substitute. It alters language in a bill or another amendment but does not replace the entire text of either one.

Permanent Appropriation An appropriation that remains continuously available, without current action or renewal by Congress, under the terms of a previously enacted authorization or appropriation law. One such appropriation provides for payment of interest on the public debt and another the salaries of members of Congress.

Permanent Authorization An authorization without a time limit. It usually does not specify any limit on the funds that may be appropriated for the agency, program, or activity that it authorizes, leaving such amounts to the discretion of the appropriations committees and the two houses. A permanent authorization continues in effect unless, or until, Congress changes or terminates it.

Permanent Staff Committee staff authorized by rule or law, as distinguished from temporary or investigative staff authorized by annual or biennial resolutions. All but two House standing committees may appoint a maximum of thirty permanent staff (eighteen professional and twelve clerical staff). The House Appropriations and Budget committees may appoint any number of staff, subject to the amount of funds appropriated for them in the annual legislative branch appropriations act. The Senate eliminated the distinction between permanent and investigative staff in 1981.

Personal Privilege A question of privilege relating to members individually.

Personally Obnoxious (or Objectionable) A characterization a senator sometimes applies to a president's nominee for a federal office in that senator's state to justify his or her opposition to the nomination.

Petition A formal plea from a citizen, group, or organization that asks Congress to take some legislative action or oppose an action.

Pigeonhole In a committee, to put a measure aside indefinitely with the intention of ignoring it. Thousands of bills are pigeonholed in every Congress for a variety of reasons.

Pipeline Appropriations obligated in one fiscal year that will not be spent until some year in the future are often said to be in the pipeline.

Pocket Veto The indirect veto of a bill as a result of the president withholding approval of it until after Congress has adjourned sine die. A bill the president does not sign, but does not formally veto while Congress is in session, automatically becomes a law ten days (excluding Sundays) after it is received. But if Congress adjourns its annual session during that ten-day period, the measure dies even if the president does not formally veto it.

Point of No Quorum A point of order that a quorum is not present. It is used in the House but rarely in the Senate where the practice is to suggest the absence of a quorum.

Point of Order A parliamentary term used in committee and on the floor to object to an alleged violation of a rule and to demand that the chair enforce the rule. The objecting member must explain the nature of the violation. A point of order immediately halts the proceedings until the chair decides whether the contention is valid.

With some exceptions in the House, a member may appeal the chair's ruling. Appeals are rarely demanded in the House and even more rarely upheld. They are demanded more often in the Senate and are occasionally successful.

Policy Committees The political party committees in each house that review legislative proposals and provide recommendations or advice on party action and policy. Majority party policy committees advise their leaders on the scheduling of measures for floor action. In the House, these functions are performed for the Democratic Party by its Steering and Policy Committee.

Popular Titles The informal, unofficial names by which bills and laws are better known. For example, the Balanced Budget and Emergency Deficit Control Act of 1985 is usually referred to as the Gramm-Rudman-Hollings Act or merely as Gramm-Rudman.

Pork *or* Pork Barrel Legislation Pejorative terms for federal appropriations, bills, or policies that provide funds to benefit a legislator's district or state, with the implication that the legislator presses for enactment of such benefits to ingratiate himself or herself with constituents rather than on the basis of an impartial, objective assessment of need or merit.

The terms are often applied to such benefits as new parks, post offices, dams, canals, bridges, roads, water projects, sewage treatment plants, and public works of any kind, as well as demonstration projects, research grants, and relocation of government facilities. Funds released by the president for various kinds of benefits or government contracts approved by him allegedly for political purposes are also sometimes referred to as pork.

Postcloture Filibuster A filibuster conducted after the Senate invokes cloture. It employs an array of procedural tactics rather than lengthy speeches to delay final action.

The Senate curtailed the postcloture filibuster's effectiveness by closing a variety of loopholes in the cloture rule in 1979 and 1986, principally by fixing a time limitation on all proceedings following a Senate vote to invoke cloture. Moreover, under the Senate's precedents, the chair may rule dilatory and nongermane amendments out of order on his own initiative once cloture is invoked.

Postpone A motion to postpone a proposal indefinitely kills it. Postponing to a day certain brings the proposal back for consideration on the specified day. Both motions are debatable.

Power of the Purse A reference to the constitutional power Congress has over legislation to raise revenue and appropriate monies from the Treasury. Article I, Section 8, states that Congress "shall have Power To lay and collect Taxes, Duties, Imposts and Excises, [and] to pay the Debts...." Section 9 declares: "No Money shall be drawn from the Treasury, but in Consequence of Appropriations made by Law...."

Preamble Introductory language describing the reasons for and intent of a measure, sometimes called a whereas clause. It occasionally appears in joint, concurrent, and simple resolutions but rarely in bills. In a bill it is placed before the enacting clause, in a joint resolution before the resolving clause, and in other resolutions above the text. Like other parts of a measure, preambles may be amended.

Precedence The order in which amendments and other motions may be offered and acted on.

Precedent A previous ruling on a parliamentary matter or a long-standing practice or custom of a house. Before a presiding officer makes a ruling, he or she is expected to consider prior rulings on the same, similar, or analogous questions. Precedents serve to control arbitrary rulings and serve as the common law of a house. Each house compiles and publishes its precedents from time to time.

President of the Senate The vice president of the United States in his constitutional role as presiding officer of the Senate. Senators address him and his surrogates as "Mr. President." The Constitution permits the vice president to cast a vote in the Senate only to break a tie, but he is not required to do so. This vote is sometimes called a casting vote. The Senate usually authorizes the vice president, by unanimous consent, to appoint senators to conference committees and to some commissions and boards, but he normally appoints those recommended by the Senate's party leaders or by the chairman and ranking minority member of the committee with jurisdiction over the measure.

Modern vice presidents usually preside only when their vote may be needed, on ceremonial occasions, or to rule on some crucial procedural questions. The president pro tempore or a senator designated by him presides over the Senate during the vice president's frequent absences.

President Pro Tempore Under the Constitution, an officer elected by the Senate to preside over it during the absence of the vice president of the United States. Often referred to as "the pro tem," he is usually the majority party senator with the longest continuous service in the chamber and also, by virtue of his seniority, a committee chairman. When attending to committee and other duties, the president pro tempore appoints other senators to preside. Whoever presides is formally addressed as Mr. or Madam President. In 1890, the Senate decided that a president pro tempore should continue in that office until it determines otherwise.

Presiding Officer In a formal meeting, the individual authorized to maintain order and decorum, recognize members to speak or offer motions, and apply and interpret the chamber's rules, precedents, and practices. The Speaker of the House and the president of the Senate are the chief presiding officers in their respective houses.

Previous Question A nondebatable motion which, when agreed to by majority vote, usually cuts off further debate, prevents the offering of additional amendments, and brings the pending matter to an immediate vote. It is a major debate-limiting device in the House; it is not permitted in the Committee of the Whole or in the Senate. If the previous question is ordered on a debatable proposal before any debate has occurred on it, the proposal may be debated for forty minutes.

Printed Amendment (1) In the House, an amendment printed in the *Congressional Record* at least one day before it is offered in the Committee of the Whole; sometimes called a previously noticed amendment. Unlike other amendments, a printed amendment offered to a part of a bill on which the committee has closed debate may nevertheless be debated by its sponsor for five minutes, and another member may speak five minutes in opposition. No further debate is permitted.

(2) In the Senate, an amendment submitted for printing in the *Congressional Record* under the heading Amendments Submitted. The printing gives other senators an opportunity to examine the amendment but gives it no special parliamentary standing or status.

Private Bill A bill that applies to one or more specified persons, corporations, institutions, or other entities, usually to grant relief when no other legal remedy is available to them. Many private bills deal with claims against the federal government, immigration and naturalization cases, and land titles. The title of a private bill usually begins, "For the relief of...."

Congress has considerably reduced its private claims workload since the mid-nineteenth century by authorizing executive branch agencies to settle them. Occasionally, Congress refers private claims to the U.S. Court of Claims for advisory findings.

Private Calendar Commonly used title for a calendar in the House reserved for private bills and resolutions favorably reported by committees. The private calendar is officially called the Calendar of the Committee of the Whole House. The calendar must be called on the first Tuesday of the month unless dispensed with by a two-thirds vote; it may also be called on the third Tuesday of the month at the Speaker's discretion.

Private Law A private bill enacted into law. Private laws are numbered in the same fashion as public laws.

Privilege An attribute of a motion, measure, report, question, or proposition that gives it priority status for consideration. That status may come from provisions of the Constitution, standing rules, precedents, or statutory rules. Privileged questions are those given priority in the order of business; questions of privilege concern the rights and safety of a house and of its individual members. Privileged motions and motions to bring up privileged questions are not debatable.

Privilege of the Floor In addition to the members of a house, certain individuals are admitted to its floor while it is in session. The rules of the two houses differ somewhat, but both extend the privilege to the president and vice president, Supreme Court justices, cabinet members, state governors, former members of that house, members of the other house, certain officers and officials of Congress, certain staff of that house in the discharge of official duties, and the chambers' former parliamentarians. They also allow access to a limited number of committee and members' staff when their presence is necessary. House customs and practices permit selected individuals who do not have floor privileges to go to the floor during joint meetings of Congress.

Privileged Business Business that has priority over the daily order of business; also called privileged interruptions in the House. Some items of business are privileged in both houses, but the House confers that status on more items than does the Senate.

Privileged Report In the House, a committee report that may be filed from the floor at any time because it deals with a privileged measure or matter. A report's privilege may stem from a constitutional provision, as in the case of vetoed measures and impeachment proceedings, or it may be provided in the standing rules.

Pro Forma Amendment In the House, an amendment that ostensibly proposes to change a measure or another amendment by moving "to strike the last word" or "to strike the requisite number of words." A member offers it not to make any actual change in the measure or amendment but only to obtain time for debate.

Pro forma amendments are permitted in the House of Representatives under the five-minute rule, either in the Committee of the Whole or in the House as in Committee of the Whole, but not in the Senate. In modern practice, pro forma amendments are not put to a vote and are considered as withdrawn when the time has expired of the member who has offered one.

Pro Forma Session A brief meeting of a house held to satisfy the constitutional requirement that it must obtain the consent of the other house if it adjourns for more than three days. It is understood that little or no business will be conducted during such meetings because most members are absent. The unofficial record for the shortest session of a house is two seconds, set by the Senate in 1963.

Pro Tem A common reference to the president pro tempore of the Senate or, occasionally, to a Speaker pro tempore.

Procedures The methods of conducting business in a deliberative body. The procedures of each house are governed first by applicable provisions of the Constitution, then by its standing rules and orders, precedents, traditional practices, and any statutory rules that apply to it. The authority of the houses to adopt rules in addition to those specified in the Constitution is derived from Article I, Section 5, Clause 2 of the Constitution, which states: "Each House may determine the Rules of its Proceedings...."

Program, Project, or Activity (PPA) An element within a federal budget account. In annually appropriated accounts, PPAs are defined by the appropriations acts and their accompanying reports and documentation. For accounts not funded by annual appropriations, PPAs are defined by the program listings in the program and financing schedule in the president's budget.

Proxy Voting The practice of permitting a member to cast the vote of an absent colleague in addition to his own vote. Proxy voting is prohibited on the floors of the House and Senate, but both houses permit their committees to authorize proxy voting, and most do.

When authorized by a House committee, members must submit signed proxy authorizations limited to a specific measure, amendments to it, and motions relating to it. General proxies on procedural motions are also permitted.

The Senate rule declares that "proxies may not be voted when the absent member has not been informed of the matter on which he is being recorded and has not affirmatively requested that he be so recorded."

Public Bill A bill dealing with general legislative matters having national applicability or applying to the federal government or to a class of persons, groups, or organizations.

Public Debt Federal government debt incurred by the Treasury or the Federal Financing Bank by the sale of securities to the public or borrowings from a federal fund or account.

Public Law A public bill or joint resolution enacted into law. It is cited by the letters P.L. followed by a hyphenated number. The digits before the hyphen indicate the number of the Congress in which it was enacted; the digits after the hyphen indicate its position in the numerical sequence of public measures that became law during that Congress. For example, the Budget Enforcement Act of 1990 became P.L. 101-508 because it was the 508th measure in that sequence for the 101st Congress.

Put the Question The procedure for initiating a vote on a proposal. The chair puts the question to a vote when all the time for debate on the question has expired, when no member seeks recognition to debate it further, or when no debate is permitted.

Q

Question A parliamentary term for a pending proposition, such as a measure, motion, or amendment when the chair puts it to a vote by stating, "The question is on the [type of proposition]."

Question of Privilege Two classes of privileged questions, one relating to a house collectively, the other to members individually. A House rule defines the first, called privilege of the House, as questions affecting the rights of the House and the safety, dignity, and integrity of its proceedings. The second, called personal privilege, refers to questions affecting the rights, reputation, and conduct of individual members in their representative capacity only. Generally, both types of questions have precedence over all others in the House except motions to adjourn.

Quorum The minimum number of members required to be present for the transaction of business. Under the Constitution, a quorum in each house is a majority of its members: 218 in the House and 51 in the Senate when there are no vacancies. By House rule, a quorum in the Committee of the Whole is 100. In practice, both houses usually assume a quorum is present even if it is not, unless a member makes a point of no quorum in the House or suggests the absence of a quorum in the Senate. Consequently, each house transacts much of its business, and even passes bills, when only a few members are present.

A majority quorum must actually be present in a Senate committee when it reports a measure or recommendation. The same rule applied to House committees until 1993 when it was changed in two respects. First, a majority quorum need not actually be present during a roll-call vote to report; the only requirement is that a majority of the committee's members must respond to the vote. Thus, members who have voted need not remain to establish the physical presence of a majority quorum during the vote; it is sufficient that the records of the committee establish that a majority of its members responded. This is sometimes referred to as a "rolling quorum" or "drop-by voting."

Second, on measures reported by unanimous consent or voice votes, no point of order against the measure on the ground that a majority quorum was not present during such actions is permitted on the House floor unless such a point of order was made in the committee at the time of such action.

As few as one-third of a committee's members may transact other business. Senate committees may fix a number less than one-third for taking sworn testimony; House committees may take testimony with a quorum of two.

When the House chooses a president, the Constitution requires a quorum of at least one member each from two-thirds of the states. The Constitution also mandates a quorum of two-thirds of the Senate when that body elects a vice president.

Quorum Call A procedure for determining whether a quorum is present in a chamber. In the Senate, a clerk calls the roll (roster) of senators. The House usually employs its electronic voting system.

R

Ramseyer Rule A House rule that requires a committee's report on a bill or joint resolution to show the changes the measure, and any committee amendments to it, would make in existing law. That part of the report is often called "the Ramseyer."

The rule requires the report to present the text of any statutory provision that would be repealed and a comparative print showing, through typographical devices such as stricken-through type or italics, other changes in existing law.

The rule, adopted in 1929, is named after its sponsor, Rep. Christian W. Ramseyer (R-Iowa). The Senate's analogous rule is the Cordon Rule.

Randolph Rule A reference to a Senate resolution adopted in 1984 that requires senators to vote from their seats. Sen. Jennings Randolph (D-W.Va.) sponsored the resolution.

Rank or Ranking A member's position on the list of his party's members on a committee or subcommittee. When first assigned to a committee, a member is placed at the bottom of the list, then moves up as those above leave the committee. On subcommittees, however, a member's rank may not have anything to do with the length of his service on it.

Ranking Member (1) Most often a reference to the minority member with the highest ranking on a committee or subcommittee.

(2) A reference to the majority member next in rank to the chairman or to the highest

ranking majority member present at a committee or subcommittee meeting.

Ranking Minority Member The member whose name appears at the head of the list of minority members on a committee or subcommittee. The ranking minority member usually appoints the minority staff, acts as minority floor manager on committee measures, and recommends minority members for appointment as conferees on such measures.

In the House, the rules of the Republican Conference prohibit its members from serving as ranking minority member on more than one committee or, except with conference approval, on more than one subcommittee. Senate Republicans may hold that position on one standing and one joint committee.

On December 8, 1992, the House Republican Conference adopted a rule that prohibits any of its members from holding any full committee's ranking position for more than six consecutive years; subcommittee positions are not affected. The rule went into effect in 1993 and is not retroactive.

Ratification (1) The president's formal act of promulgating a treaty after the Senate has approved it. The resolution of ratification agreed to by the Senate is the procedural vehicle by which the Senate gives its consent to ratification.

(2) A state legislature's act in approving a proposed constitutional amendment. Such an amendment becomes effective when ratified by three-fourths of the states.

Reading for Amendment In the Committee of the Whole, the House practice of completing action on all amendments to a section or paragraph of a measure, after a clerk has read or designated it, before permitting amendments to the next section or paragraph. A full reading of a section's text is often waived by unanimous consent or by a special rule from the Rules Committee.

The Senate's rules do not require that a measure be read for amendment; therefore, senators may offer amendments to any part of a measure and in any order. The same is true in the House when it takes up a measure in the House as in Committee of the Whole.

Reading of Amendments Both houses require that a clerk read each amendment in full to the chamber before the amendment is debated, amended, or brought to a vote. The reading is often waived by unanimous consent or by a special rule from the Rules Committee in the House.

Readings of Bills and Resolutions Both houses require three so-called readings of bills and joint resolutions before passage, but in the House the first and third readings are by the title of the measure only and in the Senate all three are by title only. The House requires a complete second reading but usually dispenses with it by unanimous consent for a measure considered only in the House or by special rule for measures considered in the Committee of the Whole.

Reappropriation Congressional action that permits all or part of the unobligated portion of an appropriation that has expired, or would otherwise expire, to remain available for obligation for the same or different purposes.

Recede A motion by a house to withdraw from its previous position during the process of amendments between the houses. It may recede from its amendment or from its disagreement to an amendment of the other house. In the latter case, it can simply concur in the amendment or concur with a further amendment to it.

Recess (1) A temporary interruption or suspension of a meeting of a chamber or committee. Unlike an adjournment, a recess does not end a legislative day. Because the Senate often recesses from one calendar day to another, its legislative day may extend over several calendar days, weeks, or even months. A motion to recess in the Senate takes precedence over most other motions and is not debatable.

In the House, an ordinary motion to recess has no special privilege; under a rule adopted in 1991, however, the Speaker may entertain a nondebatable motion authorizing him to declare a recess, and that motion has equal privilege with a motion to adjourn. In addition, under a rule adopted in 1993, the Speaker is authorized to declare a recess "for a short time" when no question is pending before the House.

(2) A period of adjournment for more than three days to a day certain, especially over a holiday or in August during odd-numbered years.

Recess Appointment A presidential appointment to a vacant federal position made after the Senate has adjourned sine die or has adjourned or recessed for more than thirty days. If the president submits the recess appointee's nomination during the next session of the Senate, that individual can continue to serve until the end of the session even though the Senate might have rejected the nomination.

Recognition Permission by the presiding officer to a member to speak or propose a procedural action. A member seeking recognition must rise and address the chair, but may not do so while another member holds the floor unless that member has violated a rule.

Recommit To send a measure back to the committee that reported it; sometimes called a straight motion to recommit to distinguish it from a motion to recommit with instructions. A successful motion to recommit kills the measure unless it is accompanied by instructions. The motion is allowed in the Senate and the House but not in Committee of the Whole. In the Senate, a motion to recommit a measure may be offered any time before the measure's passage or adoption. In the House, the motion may be offered just before the vote on final passage or adoption.

Recommit with Instructions To send a measure back to a committee with instructions to take some action on it. Invariably in the House and often in the Senate, when the motion recommits to a standing committee, the instructions require the committee to report the measure "forthwith" with specified amendments. In that case, the majority floor manager immediately reports it back to the chamber with the required amendments; the committee does not physically receive the measure or convene to act on it. Once reported, the amendments must still be voted on by the chamber. The motion is not allowed in the Committee of the Whole.

In the Senate, the motion to recommit with instructions and to report forthwith without any amendments has the effect of stripping the measure of all floor amendments previously agreed to. Accordingly, unanimous consent agreements often restrict its use and it is rarely offered.

Reconciliation A procedure for changing existing revenue and spending laws to bring total federal revenues and spending within the limits established in a budget resolution.

Congress has applied reconciliation chiefly to revenues and mandatory spending programs, especially entitlements. Discretionary spending is controlled through annual appropriation bills.

Reconsider a Vote A parliamentary practice that gives a house one opportunity to review its action on a motion, amendment, measure, or any other proposition. Killing a motion to reconsider an action by laying the motion on the table makes that action final and blocks any future attempt to reverse it.

Recorded Vote Generally, any vote in which members are recorded by name for or against a measure; also called a record vote or roll-call vote. The only recorded vote in the Senate is a vote by the yeas and nays and is commonly called a roll-call vote.

Recorded Vote by Clerks A voting procedure in the House where members pass through the appropriate "aye" or "no" aisle in the chamber and cast their votes by depositing a signed green (yea) or red (no) card in a ballot box. These votes are tabulated by clerks and reported to the chair. The electronic voting system is much more convenient and has largely supplanted this procedure.

Redistricting The redrawing of congressional district boundaries within a state after a decennial census. Redistricting may be required to re-equalize district populations or to accommodate an increase or decrease in the number of a state's House seats that might have resulted from the decennial apportionment.

The state governments determine the district lines, but they are subject both to Supreme Court decisions that district populations should be as nearly equal as practicable and to federal laws that prohibit districting intended to dilute the voting power of minorities or that produce discriminatory results.

Referral The assignment of a measure to one or more committees for consideration.

Regulatory Impact Statement An evaluation of the regulatory impact of a proposed bill or joint resolution. It is required to appear in Senate committee reports.

A regulatory impact statement must include: (1) an estimate of the number and types of individuals and businesses that would be regulated by the measure; (2) the economic impact of the measure on individuals, consumers, and businesses; (3) the measure's impact on personal privacy; and (4) how much additional paperwork the measure would require and the paperwork costs in time and money.

Report A committee document that accompanies a reported measure. It describes the measure, the committee's views on it, its costs, and the changes it proposes to make in existing law; it also includes certain impact statements. These reports are required in the House; although they are optional in the Senate, its committees usually provide them.

A committee document submitted to its parent chamber that describes the results of an investigation or other study or provides information it is required to provide by rule or law.

Representative An elected and duly sworn member of the House of Representatives who is entitled to vote in the chamber. The Constitution requires that a representative be at least twenty-five years old, a citizen of the United States for at least seven years, and an inhabitant of the state from which he or she is elected. Customarily, the member resides in the district he or she represents. Representatives are elected in even-numbered years to two-year terms that begin the following January.

Reprimand A formal condemnation of a member for misbehavior, considered a milder reproof than censure. The House of Representatives first used it in 1976 when it approved a resolution accepting a reprimand recommendation reported by its Standards of Official Conduct Committee. Adoption of the report usually constitutes the reprimand, but the Speaker can administer it verbally. The Senate has not used the term.

Rescind A seldom used motion to annul or invalidate a previously taken action. On rare occasions, the House has nullified proceedings by rescinding the records of them in the *Journal* and both houses have rescinded or expunged entries in the *Journal*s of preceding Congresses.

Rescission A provision of law that repeals previously enacted budget authority in whole or in part. Under the Impoundment Control Act of 1974, the president can impound such funds by sending a message to Congress requesting one or more rescissions and the reasons for doing so. If Congress does not pass a rescission bill for the programs requested by the president within forty-five days of continuous session after receiving the message, the president must make the funds available for obligation and expenditure. If the president does not, the comptroller general of the United States is authorized to bring suit to compel the release of those funds. A rescission bill may rescind all, part, or none of an amount proposed by the president, and may rescind funds the president has not impounded.

Reservation A statement added to a Senate resolution of ratification of a treaty. It usually limits the obligations of the United States under the treaty.

Reserving a Point of Order In the House, a member's declaration that he may make a point of order against a pending matter at some indefinite future time. By reserving a point of order, a member attempts to circumvent the requirement that points of order must be made against a matter before debate on that matter begins.

The practice of reserving a point of order is not followed in the Senate because a senator is allowed to make a point of order against a matter at any time it is under consideration.

Reserving the Right to Object A member's declaration that at some indefinite future time he or she may object to a unanimous consent request. It is an attempt to circumvent the requirement that a member may prevent such an action only by objecting immediately after it is proposed.

Resident Commissioner from Puerto Rico A nonvoting member of the House of Representatives, elected to a four-year term. The resident commissioner has the same status and privileges as delegates. Like the delegates, the resident commissioner may not vote in the House, but a rule adopted in 1993 allows him to vote in the Committee of the Whole.

Resolution (1) A simple resolution; that is, a nonlegislative measure effective only in the house in which it is proposed and not requiring concurrence by the other chamber or approval by the president. Simple resolutions are designated H. Res. in the House and S. Res. in the Senate and are consecutively numbered in the order of their introduction during a two-year Congress. Simple resolutions express nonbinding opinions on policies or issues or deal with the internal affairs or prerogatives of a house.

Resolution of Inquiry A resolution—usually simple rather than concurrent—calling on the president or the head of an executive agency to provide specific information or papers to one or both houses.

Resolution of Ratification The Senate vehicle for agreeing to a treaty. The constitutionally mandated vote of two-thirds of the senators present and voting applies to the adoption of this resolution. However, it may also contain amendments, reservations, declarations, or understandings that the Senate had previously added to it by majority vote.

Resolving Clause The first section of a joint resolution that begins "Resolved by the Senate and House of Representatives of the United States of America in Congress assembled...." This language gives legal force to the measure when approved by Congress and signed by the president or when a veto is overridden by Congress.

Revenue Legislation Measures that levy new taxes or tariffs or change existing ones. Under Article I, Section 7, Clause 1 of the Constitution, the House of Representatives originates federal revenue measures, but the Senate can propose amendments to them. The House Ways and Means Committee and the Senate Finance Committee have jurisdiction over such measures, with a few minor exceptions.

Revise and Extend One's Remarks A unanimous consent request to publish in the *Congressional Record* a statement a member did not deliver on the floor, a longer statement than the one made on the floor, or miscellaneous extraneous material. Members frequently make such requests, and these are rarely objected to, because debate time is limited in the House.

Revolving Fund A trust fund or account whose income remains available to finance its continuing operations without any fiscal year limitation.

Riddick's Senate Procedure A single-volume digest of Senate precedents, procedures, and practices originally compiled by Floyd M. Riddick, a parliamentarian emeritus. The fourth edition, revised and edited by Alan S. Frumin, parliamentarian of the Senate, was published as a Senate document in 1992.

Rider Congressional slang for an amendment unrelated or extraneous to the subject matter of the measure to which it is attached. Riders often contain proposals that are less likely to become law on their own merits as separate bills, either because of opposition in the committee of jurisdiction, resistance in the other house, or the probability of a presidential veto.

Riders are more common in the Senate, where the rules permit unrelated amendments on most legislation, than in the House, where a rule requires amendments to be germane. Nevertheless, House bills often carry riders because no point of order is made against them or because points of order are waived by a special rule.

Riders sometimes take the guise of limitation provisions in general appropriation bills.

Rise In congressional jargon, a committee is said to rise when it ends a meeting. When a Committee of the Whole completes its work on a measure, it rises and its chairman immediately reports its recommendations to the full House.

Roll Call A call of the roll to determine whether a quorum is present, to establish a quorum, or to vote on a question.

Usually, the House uses its electronic voting system for a roll call, but when the system is malfunctioning the Speaker directs the clerk to read the names. The Senate does not have an electronic voting system; its roll is always called by a clerk. After the entire roll has been called, the clerk calls the names of those who did not respond and the names of members who indicate they now wish to respond.

Before the chair has announced the result of a roll-call vote in the Senate, senators are permitted to ask how they are recorded on the vote and to change the way they are recorded, if they so desire. Sometimes, a number of senators rise in turn to ask how they are recorded in order to delay the announcement of the vote's result until one or more absent senators can come to the floor and cast their votes. Representatives can change their votes by presenting themselves in the well of the House and seeking recognition for that purpose before the chair has announced the result of the vote.

Rolling Quorum The method by which each house complies with the requirements for establishing the "presence" of a quorum during a quorum call or recorded vote without requiring the actual presence of a majority of its members in the chamber at the same time. Under this practice, it is sufficient that the required number of members arrive in the chamber and record their presence at some time during the call or vote, after which they may leave.

Rule (1) A permanent regulation that a house adopts to govern its conduct of business, its procedures, its internal organization, behavior of its members, regulation of its facilities, duties of an officer, or some other subject it chooses to govern in that form. In addition to its standing rules, a house is subject to precedents, constitutional rules, statutory rules, standing orders, and, in the House of Representatives, certain rules in *Jefferson's Manual.*

Under the Constitution, each house determines the rules of its proceedings, an authority called the rulemaking power. Generally, when two or more rules are in conflict, the most recently adopted rule is followed.

(2) In the House, a privileged simple resolution reported by the Rules Committee that provides methods and conditions for floor consideration of a measure or, rarely, several measures.

Rulemaking Power The constitutional authority of each house to determine the rules of its proceedings. In accordance with this authority, a house may change its rules at any time, may change any statutory rule as it applies to that house, or may adopt a rule that supersedes a statutory rule.

S

Scope of Differences The limits within which a conference committee is permitted to resolve the disagreements between the two houses on a measure.

Second Degree Amendment An amendment to an amendment in the first degree. It is usually a perfecting amendment.

Second Reading A required reading of a bill or joint resolution to a chamber: in the Senate, by title only before referral to a committee; in the House, in full before floor consideration in the House or in Committee of the Whole. The House usually dispenses with the full reading before consideration in the House by unanimous consent and in the Committee of the Whole by a special rule.

Secret *or* Closed Session A session of either house that is held behind closed doors to discuss business deemed to require secrecy. Only members and necessary staff may attend.

Secretary of the Senate The chief administrative and budgetary officer of the Senate. The secretary manages a wide range of functions that support the operation of the Senate as an organization as well as those functions necessary to its legislative process.

Section A subdivision of a bill or statute. By law, a section must be numbered and, as nearly as possible, contain "a single proposition of enactment."

When a measure is not divided into titles, its sections are numbered 1, 2, 3, and so on. Within a title, the first one or two digits of each section's number corresponds with its title's roman number: Title I begins with section 101, title II with section 201, and so forth.

Select *or* Special Committee A committee established by a resolution in either house for a special purpose and, usually, for a limited time. Most select and special committees are assigned specific investigations or studies, but are not authorized to report measures to their chambers. During the past several decades, however, both houses created several permanent select and special committees and gave legislative reporting authority to a few of them: the Ethics and the Indian Affairs committees in the Senate and the Intelligence committees in both houses.

There is no substantive difference between a select and a special committee.

Self-Executing Rule A special rule from the House Rules Committee stipulating that upon the adoption of the rule, the House is deemed to have passed a measure, adopted an amendment, or taken some other action. The rule precludes a separate vote.

Senate The house of Congress in which each state is represented by two senators; each senator has one vote. Article V of the Constitution declares that "No State, without its Consent, shall be deprived of its equal Suffrage in the Senate." The Constitution also gives the Senate equal legislative power with the House of Representatives. Although the Senate is prohibited from originating revenue measures, and as a matter of practice it does not originate appropriation measures, it can amend both.

Only the Senate can give or withhold consent to treaties and nominations from the president. It also acts as a court to try impeachments by the House and elects the vice president when no candidate receives a majority of the electoral votes. It is often referred to as "the upper body," but not by members of the House.

Senate Manual The handbook of the Senate's standing rules and orders and the laws and other regulations that apply to the Senate, usually published once each Congress. It also contains several historical documents, including the Constitution, and lists of all senators and other Senate officials from the First Congress to date.

Senator A duly sworn elected or appointed member of the Senate. The Constitution requires that a senator be at least thirty years old, a citizen of the United States for at least nine years, and an inhabitant of the state from which he or she is elected. Senators are usually elected in even-numbered years to six-year terms that begin the following January.

Senatorial Courtesy The Senate's practice of declining to confirm a presidential nominee for an office in the state of a senator of the president's party unless that senator approves. Sometimes called "the courtesy of the Senate," the practice is a customary one and not always adhered to. A senator sometimes invokes the custom by declaring that the nominee is personally obnoxious or personally objectionable to him.

Senior Senator Of the two senators from a state, the one with the longer continuous service in the Senate.

Seniority The priority, precedence, or status accorded members according to the length of their continuous service in a house or on a committee.

Seniority Loss A type of punishment that reduces a member's seniority on his or her committees, including the loss of chairmanships. Party caucuses in both houses have occasionally imposed such punishment on their members, for example, for publicly supporting candidates of the other party.

Seniority Rule The customary practice, rather than a rule, of assigning the chairmanship of a committee to the majority party member who has served on the committee for the longest continuous period of time.

Seniority System A collection of long-standing customary practices under which members with longer continuous service than their colleagues in their house or on their committees receive various kinds of preferential treatment. Although some of the practices are no longer as rigidly observed as in the past, they still pervade the organization and procedures of Congress.

Usually, the majority party member with the greatest seniority on a committee serves as its chairman, although in recent decades the House Democratic Caucus has occasionally chosen members with less seniority to replace a chairman or to fill a vacant chairmanship. Committee members are ranked among their party colleagues according to their committee seniority, and chairmen usually recognize them to question witnesses and to offer motions and amendments in the order of their ranking. The parties also take seniority in their houses into account when filling vacancies on committee rosters. Committee seniority is also a factor in the selection of subcommittee chairmen and of conferees.

Sequestration A procedure for canceling budgetary resources—that is, money available for obligation or spending—to enforce budget limitations established in law. Sequestered funds are no longer available for obligation or expenditure.

Sergeant at Arms The officer in each house responsible for maintaining order, security, and decorum in its wing of the Capitol, including the chamber and its galleries. In the House of Representatives, the mace is the symbol of this office. The Senate sergeant at arms also performs the duties of doorkeeper. Although elected by their respective houses, both sergeants at arms are invariably the candidates of the majority party.

Session (1) The annual series of meetings of a Congress. Under the Constitution, Congress must assemble at least once a year at noon on January 3 unless it appoints a different day by law.

(2) The meetings of Congress or of one house convened by the president under his constitutional authority, called a special session.

(3) A house is said to be in session during the period of a day when it is meeting.

Seven-Day Rule (1) In both houses, if a chairman fails to call a special meeting of a committee to be held within seven calendar days after three committee members have requested it, a majority of the committee can call such a meeting.

(2) In both houses, a committee's report on a measure it has approved must be filed with the parent house within seven calendar days after a majority of the committee's members has signed a request for that purpose and submitted it to the committee's clerk. Before this rule was adopted in 1970, committee chairmen sometimes refused to file reports on measures they disliked.

(3) In the House, if a member who has reported a special rule from the Rules Committee does not call it up within the next seven legislative days, any member of the committee can call it up as a question of privilege one day after that member announces the intention to do so.

(4) If the House has adopted a special rule making it in order to consider a measure and if no motion to consider it has been offered within seven days, the Speaker may recognize any authorized member of the committee that reported it to offer that motion.

(5) A motion to discharge a committee must remain on the discharge calendar at least seven days before it may be called up for consideration.

Severability (*or* Separability) Clause Language stating that if any particular provisions of a measure are declared invalid by the courts, the remaining provisions shall still be in effect.

Sine Die Without fixing a day for a future meeting. An adjournment sine die signifies the end of an annual or special session of Congress.

Sit (1) A house or a committee is said to sit when it is meeting. The rules of both houses forbid their committees to sit during certain proceedings of their parent bodies unless they receive special leave.

(2) To hold a committee or subcommittee assignment. A senator, for example, must sit on two committees.

Slip Law The first official publication of a measure that has become law. It is published separately in unbound, single-sheet form or pamphlet form. A slip law usually is available two or three days after the date of the law's enactment.

Speak Out of Order To speak on a subject not relevant or germane to the matter under consideration when germane debate is required. To speak out of order requires unanimous consent. A member who speaks out of order without unanimous consent may be asked to sit down and be silent.

Speaker The presiding officer of the House of Representatives and the leader of its majority party. The Speaker is selected by the majority party and formally elected by the House at the beginning of each Congress. Although the Constitution does not require the Speaker to be a member of the House, in fact, all Speakers have been members.

As presiding officer, the Speaker maintains order in the House, manages the flow of legislation to the floor, and has numerous administrative responsibilities, including general control of the House side of the Capitol.

As party leader, the Speaker chairs the party's

Committee on Committees, plans the party's legislative strategy, and negotiates committee party ratios with the minority leader. In addition, the Speaker is second to the vice president in the line of succession to the presidency.

Speaker Pro Tempore A member of the House who is designated as the temporary presiding officer by the Speaker or elected by the House to that position during the Speaker's absence.

Speaker's Table The Speaker is required to dispose of certain communications received by the House of Representatives from the executive branch and from the Senate, and these communications are said to be on his table. He refers most of them to the appropriate committees.

Speaker's Vote The Speaker is not required to vote, and his name is not called on a roll-call vote unless he so requests. Usually, the Speaker votes either to create a tie vote, and thereby defeat a proposal, or to break a tie in favor of a proposal. Occasionally, the Speaker also votes to emphasize the importance of a matter or his special interest in it.

Special Appropriation Bill An appropriation measure other than a general appropriation bill and therefore not subject to the rules of the authorization-appropriation process.

Special Committee Meeting A meeting convened at the request of a committee's members. In both houses, a majority of a committee's members can force the convening of such a meeting if its chairman refuses a request to call one.

Special Order A temporary regulation or directive. In the House, it is often a rule (also called a special rule) reported by the Rules Committee that provides methods for the consideration of a measure or, rarely, a class of measures. Special orders are adopted by majority vote, unanimous consent, or occasionally by suspension of the rules.

A Senate rule requires a two-thirds vote to adopt special orders fixing a day and time for the consideration of legislative proposals, but in practice the Senate uses unanimous consent agreements for those purposes.

Special Order of Business In the House of Representatives, business that supplants the daily order of business, or that may do so, on specified days.

Special Order Speech A type of special order that, by unanimous consent, permits a member to address his house on any subject when it is not considering business. Unanimous consent is required because under the rules of both houses, members may be recognized to give speeches on the floor only during debate on a matter that has been brought up for consideration.

Special Session A session of Congress convened by the president, under his constitutional authority, after Congress has adjourned sine die at the end of a regular session.

Specific Pair A pairing of two absent members on opposite sides of a question. In the House text of the *Congressional Record,* their names and positions on the question appear after the vote: "Mr. Smith for, Mr. Jones against." In the Senate text, they customarily appear before the vote in the form of an announcement by the party whips. Also called a special pair or, sometimes in the Senate, a dead pair.

Spending Authority The technical term for backdoor spending. The Congressional Budget Act of 1974 defines it as borrowing authority, contract authority, and entitlement authority for which appropriation acts do not provide budget authority in advance.

Split Referral A measure divided into two or more parts; each part is referred to a different committee.

Sponsor The principal proponent and introducer of a measure or an amendment.

Staff Director The most frequently used title for the head of staff of a committee or subcommittee. On some committees, that person is called chief of staff, clerk, chief clerk, chief counsel, general counsel, or executive director. The head of a committee's minority staff is usually called minority staff director.

Stage of Disagreement During the process of amendments between the houses, the stage reached when one house formally disagrees with an amendment proposed by the other house or insists on its own position. Ordinarily, a measure may not go to conference until this stage is reached.

Standing Committee A permanent committee established by a House or Senate standing rule or standing order. The rule also describes the subject areas on which the committee may report bills and resolutions and conduct oversight.

Standing Order A continuing regulation or directive that has the force and effect of a rule, but is not incorporated into the standing rules. The Senate's numerous standing orders, like its standing rules, continue from Congress to Congress unless changed or the order states otherwise. The House uses relatively few standing orders, and those it adopts expire at the end of a session of Congress.

Standing Rules The rules of the Senate that continue from one Congress to the next and that appear in the *Senate Manual* under the title "Standing Rules of the Senate"; and the rules of the House of Representatives that it adopts at the beginning of each new Congress, and that appear in the House Manual under "Rules of the House of Representatives, with Notes and Annotations."

Standing Vote An alternative and informal term for a division vote, during which members in favor of a proposal and then members opposed stand and are counted by the chair.

Star Print A reprint of a bill, resolution, amendment, or committee report correcting technical or substantive errors in a previous printing; so called because of the small black star that appears on the front page or cover.

Stare Decisis Literally, let the decision stand. A principle holding that a court decision should not be overturned when similar cases subsequently arise unless for compelling reasons. On the same principle, the presiding officers of each house of Congress are expected to uphold previous decisions interpreting their respective rules, but each house can overturn the chair's ruling by a successful vote on an appeal.

State of the Union Message A presidential message to Congress under the constitutional directive that he shall "from time to time give to the Congress Information of the State of the Union, and recommend to their Consideration such Measures as he shall judge necessary and expedient." Customarily, the president sends an annual State of the Union Message to Congress, usually late in January.

Statutes at Large A chronological arrangement of the laws enacted in each session of Congress. Though indexed, the laws are not arranged by subject matter nor is there an indication of how they affect or change previously enacted laws. The volumes are numbered by Congress, and the laws are cited by their volume and page number. The Gramm-Rudman-Hollings Act, for example, appears as 99 Stat. 1037.

Statutory Rules Procedural rules mandated by law for one or both houses. Though embodied in law, they are enacted under the constitutional rulemaking power of Congress; consequently, each house may at any time change a statutory rule insofar as the rule applies to that house. The manual of each house usually includes the texts of its applicable statutory rules.

Steering and Policy Committee (House) A committee of the House Democratic Caucus that advises the party leaders on legislative strategy and scheduling for floor consideration and also serves as the party's Committee on Committees.

The Republicans in both houses and the Democrats in the Senate have policy committees to develop party positions and make recommendations to their party colleagues.

Steering Committee (Senate) The committee of the Democratic Party Conference in the Senate that recommends committee assignments for party members. Its recommendations are subject to confirmation by the conference and adoption by the Senate.

Straw Vote Prohibition Under a House precedent, a member who has the floor during debate may not conduct a "straw vote" or otherwise ask for a show of support for a proposition. Only the chair may put a question to a vote.

Strike from the *Record* Expunge objectionable remarks from the *Congressional Record,* after a member's words have been taken down on a point of order.

Strike Out A motion to eliminate a part of the text of a measure, an amendment, or a treaty. A simple motion to strike out may not be amended, but while it is pending, the text it seeks to strike out may be amended.

Strike Out and Insert An amendment that replaces all or a part of the text of a measure or of another amendment.

Strike Out the Enacting (*or* Resolving) Clause A House motion whose adoption kills a bill or joint resolution. Such a motion is not directly permitted in the Committee of the Whole, but the committee can agree to a motion that it rise and report the measure to the House with the recommendation that the clause be stricken. Members frequently offer the motion merely to obtain time for debate in the Committee of the Whole rather than for its ostensible purpose. In House usage, it is called a preferential motion because it takes precedence over all other motions during the amendment stage. When offered, it rarely prevails.

Strike the Last Word A pro forma amendment that is not intended to make any actual change in the measure or amendment to which it is offered, but merely entitles a member to five minutes of debate.

Subcommittee A panel of committee members assigned a portion of the committee's jurisdiction or other functions. On legislative committees, subcommittees hold hearings, mark up legislation, and report measures to their full committee for further action; they cannot report directly to the chamber. A subcommittee's party composition usually reflects the ratio on its parent committee.

Subcommittee Assignments The subcommittees on which a member serves. Each committee determines its subcommittee assignments, subject to the rules of its house or party organizations. For certain committees, the rules limit the number of subcommittee assignments and subcommittee chairmanships a member can hold. These rules also attempt to ensure an equitable allocation of assignments to each member.

Subdivisions The Congressional Budget Act of 1974 requires that committees that are allocated budget authority and outlay amounts from a budget resolution must subdivide them by programs or subcommittees.

Subjects on the Table Business in the Senate, usually bills and resolutions, placed at the table of the chamber by unanimous consent and held there. A measure given this status is said to lie on the table and can be called up by a motion to proceed to its consideration, even though it has not been referred to a committee.

Subpoena Power The authority granted to committees by the rules of their respective houses to issue legal orders requiring individuals to appear and testify, or to produce documents pertinent to the committee's functions, or both. Persons who do not comply with subpoenas can be cited for contempt of Congress and prosecuted.

The Senate rule specifies no particular procedure for issuing subpoenas. The House rule requires a majority vote by a committee or subcommittee, provided that a quorum is present, but a committee may delegate the power to its chairman. Subpoenas can be signed by the chairman or any other member designated by the committee.

Subsidy Generally, a payment or benefit made by the federal government for which no current repayment is required. Subsidy payments may be designed to support the conduct of an economic enterprise or activity, such as ship operations, or to support certain market prices, as in the case of farm subsidies.

Substantive Law Public law other than appropriations law; sometimes called basic law or, in some contexts, existing law. It often refers to law that authorizes an agency or program.

Substitute An amendment that proposes to replace the entire text of another amendment or of a measure.

Suggest the Absence of a Quorum The phrase senators usually use to force a quorum call. Except under cloture, the Senate's presiding officer has no authority to count to determine whether a quorum is present; he must immediately direct the clerk to call the roll when a senator makes the suggestion.

Quorums are rarely present in the Senate during debate, but suggestions that a quorum is absent are frequently made not to establish a quorum but for the purpose of what some have called "constructive delay." Since the suggestion immediately suspends floor action while the roll is called, the pause gives senators time for informal discussions and negotiations or for an absent senator to arrive and offer an amendment or deliver a speech on whatever business may be pending. Aware of these purposes, the clerk calls the roll very slowly to avoid inadvertent disclosure of a quorum's absence, which would require senators to make an unnecessary trip to the floor. Once the call's purpose has been achieved, a senator asks unanimous consent that the call be dispensed with, a request invariably granted, and the Senate resumes its proceedings.

Sunset Legislation A term sometimes applied to laws authorizing the existence of agencies or programs that expire annually or at the end of some other specified period of time.

Sunshine Rules Rules requiring open committee hearings and business meetings, including markup sessions, in both houses, and also open conference committee meetings.

Super Majority A term sometimes used for a vote on a matter that requires approval by more than a simple majority of those members present and voting.

Supplemental Appropriation Bill A measure providing appropriations for use in the current fiscal year, in addition to those already provided in annual general appropriation bills. Supplemental appropriations are often for unforeseen emergencies requiring urgent expenditures that cannot be postponed until enactment of the next regular annual appropriations act.

Supplemental, Minority, and Additional Views Statements in a committee report on a measure that present dissenting or other comments of committee members.

Surplus The amount by which the government's budget receipts exceed its outlays for a given fiscal year.

Suspension of the Rules (House) An expeditious procedure for passing relatively noncontroversial or emergency measures by a two-thirds vote of those members voting, a quorum being present. Debate on a motion to suspend the rules and pass a measure is limited to forty minutes; the time is evenly divided between proponents and opponents. Members may not offer amendments from the floor, but the motion itself can include amendments. The two-thirds vote simultaneously suspends the rules and passes the measure. If the motion is not supported by the required two-thirds vote, the House has not rejected the measure involved; it has only refused to suspend the rules in order to pass it. Therefore, the measure may be considered at another time under some other procedure.

Suspension of the Rules (Senate) A procedure to set aside one or more of the Senate's rules; it is used infrequently, and then most often to suspend the rule banning legislative amendments to appropriation bills. A senator may move to suspend the rules at any time after giving one day's written notice, specifying the purpose for suspending any rule. The motion is debated under the general rules of the Senate and requires a two-thirds majority vote.

Sustained The presiding officer's affirmative ruling on a point of order. When the presiding officer makes an adverse ruling, the point of order is said to be overruled.

T

Taking Down the Words Requiring that a member's remarks be read to the chamber so that the presiding officer may determine whether they are offensive or violate the rules of that house. When any member makes a point of order against such remarks and asks that the words be "taken down," the alleged violator must immediately sit down and await the chair's decision.

Task Force A title sometimes given to a panel of members assigned to a special project, study, or investigation. The House Budget Committee uses task forces in place of subcommittees. Ordinarily, these groups do not have authority to report measures to their respective houses.

Tax Expenditure Loosely, a tax exemption or advantage, sometimes called an incentive or loophole; technically, a loss of governmental tax revenue attributable to some provision of federal tax laws that allows a special exclusion, exemption, or deduction from gross income or that provides a special credit, preferential tax rate, or deferral of tax liability. The tax exemption or advantage is usually intended to assist a certain group or to encourage a certain activity, such as the purchase of homes.

In their impact on the federal budget, tax expenditures are, in effect, subsidies provided through the tax system. Instead of making direct payments to beneficiaries, the government permits certain taxpayers to pay lower taxes than they otherwise would have to pay.

Tax Expenditure Statement A statement on the effect a measure will have on the level of tax expenditures. The statement is required to appear in the committee report on that measure.

Tax Expenditures Budget An enumeration of tax expenditures and their levels by major functional categories of the federal budget. A tax expenditures budget is required to appear in the Budget Committee's report accompanying a concurrent resolution on the budget.

Televised Proceedings Television and radio coverage of the floor proceedings of the House of

Representatives have been available since 1979 and of the Senate since 1986. They are broadcast over a coaxial cable system to all congressional offices and to some congressional agencies on channels reserved for that purpose. Coverage is also available free of charge to commercial and public television and radio broadcasters. The Cable-Satellite Public Affairs Network (C-SPAN) carries gavel-to-gavel coverage of both houses.

Teller An antiquated term for a member or clerk who counts members in certain voting or quorum-call situations.

Teller Vote A voting procedure, formerly used in the House, in which members cast their votes by passing through the center aisle to be counted, but not recorded by name, by a member from each party appointed by the chair. Members voting "aye" were counted first, followed by those members voting "no," after which the counting members reported their totals to the chair. The House deleted the procedure from its rules in 1993, but during floor discussion of the deletion a leading member stated that a teller vote would still be available in the event of a breakdown of the electronic voting system.

Temporary Staff A term sometimes applied to committee staff authorized by annual or biennial resolutions rather than by rule or law. They are also called investigative staff.

Ten-Minute Debate In the Committee of the Whole, the five-minute rule actually permits ten minutes of debate on an amendment: five minutes for its proposer and five minutes for an opponent. Moreover, debate may be extended by pro forma amendments and by unanimous consent requests.

Third Degree Amendment An amendment to a second degree amendment. Both houses prohibit such amendments.

Third Reading A required reading to a chamber of a bill or joint resolution by title only before the vote on passage. The original purpose of a third reading was to give members the opportunity to hear the full text of the measure, as it may have amended, before voting on it. In the modern practice, it has merely become a pro forma step.

Three-Day Rule (1) In the House, a committee report on a measure must be available for at least three calendar days before the measure may be considered.

(2) In the House, a conference report must be printed in the *Congressional Record* at least three calendar days before it may be considered.

(3) In both houses, a committee member is entitled to three calendar days in which to submit separate views on a measure for inclusion in the committee report.

(4) In the House, the printed hearings on a general appropriation bill must be available for at least three calendar days before the bill may be considered.

(5) In the House, measures on the consent calendar may not be called unless they have been on the calendar at least three legislative days.

(6) In both houses, a majority of a committee's members may call a special meeting of the committee if its chairman fails to do so within three calendar days after three or more of the members formally request such a meeting.

Tie Vote When the votes for and against a proposition are equal, it loses. The president of the Senate may cast a vote only to break a tie. Because the Speaker is invariably a member of the House, he is entitled to vote but usually does not. He may choose to do so to break, or create, a tie vote.

Time Limits for Voting In the House, members have a minimum of fifteen minutes to vote on recorded votes, but on clustered votes the Speaker may reduce the minimum to five minutes on the second and subsequent votes in the series.

At the beginning of recent Congresses, the Senate has adopted an order giving senators a maximum of fifteen minutes to vote when the yeas and nays are taken, but the time may be shortened by unanimous consent or lengthened by the majority and minority leaders.

Time Limits on Debate A parliamentary device that expedites the consideration of measures, motions, and other business and restricts opportunities for dilatory tactics. Virtually all debate in the House of Representatives is subject to a time limit.

The Senate's rules impose time limits in few situations, most notably under cloture, but the chamber often accepts voluntary time limits under unanimous consent agreements.

Timeliness A principle of parliamentary procedure that certain actions may be taken by a member only at a specified stage of the proceedings, after which the member loses the right to take such an action. The principle applies to actions such as the offering of motions and amendments and the making, or reserving, of points of order and objections.

Title (1) A major subdivision of a bill or act, designated by a roman numeral and usually containing legislative provisions on the same general subject. Titles are sometimes divided into subtitles as well as sections.

(2) The official name of a bill or act, also called a caption or long title. Appearing above the enacting clause, the title is usually a concise statement of the measure's subjects and purposes. Example: "A bill to improve the operation of the legislative branch of the Federal Government, and for other purposes."

(3) Some bills also have short titles that appear in the sentence immediately following the enacting clause. In the bill mentioned above, the sentence declares that the act may be cited as the "Legislative Reorganization Act of 1970." A measure sometimes provides short titles for major subdivisions that deal with unrelated or distantly related subjects. The Congressional Budget and Impoundment Control Act of 1974, for example, cites titles I through IX as the Congressional Budget Act of 1974 and title X as the Impoundment Control Act of 1974.

(4) Popular titles are the unofficial names given to some bills or acts by common usage. For example, the Balanced Budget and Emergency Deficit Control Act of 1985 (short title) is almost invariably referred to as Gramm-

Rudman (popular title). In other cases, significant legislation is popularly referred to by its title number (see definition (1) above). For example, the federal legislation that requires equality of funding for women's and men's sports in educational institutions that receive federal funds is popularly called Title IX.

Track System An occasional Senate practice that expedites legislation by dividing a day's session into two or more specific time periods, commonly called tracks, each reserved for consideration of a different measure.

Under this system, a filibuster against a particular measure can be confined to one track while the Senate continues work on several other measures.

Transfer Payment A federal government payment to which individuals or organizations are entitled under law and for which no goods or services are required in return. Payments include welfare and Social Security benefits, unemployment insurance, government pensions, and veterans' benefits. Some of these payments are indexed to the rate of inflation or some part of that rate; that is, the payments are automatically increased at that rate according to a formula established by law. These are called cost-of-living adjustments or COLAs.

Treaty A formal document containing an agreement between two or more sovereign nations. The Constitution authorizes the president to make treaties, but he must submit them to the Senate for its approval by a two-thirds vote of the senators present. Under the Senate's rules, that vote actually occurs on a resolution of ratification.

Unlike legislative measures, a treaty not yet approved does not die at the end of a Congress; it may be considered in future Congresses unless the president withdraws it or the Senate votes to return it to him.

Trust Funds Special accounts in the Treasury that receive earmarked taxes or other kinds of revenue collections, such as user fees, and from which payments are made for special purposes or to recipients who meet the requirements of the trust funds as established by law. Of the more than 150 federal government trust funds, several finance major entitlement programs, such as Social Security, Medicare, and retired federal employees' pensions. Others fund infrastructure construction and improvements, such as highways and airports.

Twenty-Day Rule A House rule that permits the chamber to discharge or instruct its conferees by majority vote if they have not reported a conference report within twenty calendar days of their appointment.

Two-Day Rule A Senate rule that prohibits floor consideration of a measure until the printed committee report on it has been available to senators for at least two calendar days. The rule may be waived by joint agreement of the majority and minority leaders. Although Senate committees are not required to provide such reports, they usually do.

Two-Hour Debate In the House, general debate on a measure called up on Calendar Wednesday is limited to two hours and is equally divided between proponents and opponents of the measure.

Two-Page Rule A regulation by the Joint Committee on Printing that requires a member to submit a cost estimate from the public printer when that member requests permission to insert extraneous material in excess of two printed pages into the *Congressional Record*.

Two-Speech Rule A Senate rule that limits senators to two speeches on any question on a single legislative day, unless the Senate grants leave for additional speeches. In practice, the Senate rarely enforces the rule.

U

Unanimous Consent Without an objection by any member. A unanimous consent request asks permission, explicitly or implicitly, to set aside one or more rules. Both houses and their committees frequently use such requests to expedite their proceedings. The Senate, in particular, relies heavily on the device because it has few other procedural methods for moving business promptly. Although members rarely object to routine unanimous consent requests, they have the right to do so and, thereby, force full compliance with the rules. Unanimous consent requests in the House came into use about 1832.

Unanimous Consent Agreement A special order approved without objection, usually to permit floor consideration of a measure under restrictive procedures; it is sometimes called a time agreement or a time limitation agreement. A unanimous consent agreement is a device to expedite legislation, frequently used in the Senate, but rarely employed in the House. Most often it is the Senate's majority leader who verbally proposes such an agreement on the floor. Once approved, it may be altered only by unanimous consent.

Unauthorized Appropriation An appropriation for a purpose not authorized in law or one that exceeds the amount authorized in law. The rules of both houses prohibit unauthorized appropriations in general appropriation bills, but permit some exceptions.

Uncontrollable Expenditures A frequently used term for federal expenditures that are mandatory under existing law and therefore cannot be controlled by the president or Congress without a change in the existing law. Uncontrollable expenditures include spending required under entitlement programs and also fixed costs, such as interest on the public debt and outlays to pay for prior-year obligations. In recent years, uncontrollables have accounted for approximately three-quarters of federal spending in each fiscal year.

Unexpended Balance The amount of budget authority that has not been spent. The obligated portion of the balance remains available until it is spend or rescinded by law. The unobligated portion of the balance remains available for spending or obligation only until the end of the period for which it was made available.

Unfinished Business A measure under consideration that is still pending when a house adjourns or recesses its daily session. If displaced by other business, unfinished business remains pending until the chamber acts on it in some fashion.

Union Calendar A calendar of the House of Representatives for bills and resolutions favorably reported by committees that raise revenue or directly or indirectly appropriate money or property. In addition to appropriation bills, measures that authorize expenditures are also placed on this calendar. The calendar's full title is the Calendar of the Committee of the Whole House on the State of the Union. A measure on it must first be considered in the Committee of the Whole before the House may act on them. Measures appear on the calendar in the order in which they were reported.

Unlimited Debate The absence of time limits on the length of speeches or on the duration of debate on most measures and motions—a distinctive feature of Senate procedure. The standing rules of the Senate impose time limits only under cloture, during a call of the calendar in the morning hour, and during an impeachment trial. In all other situations, any debatable matter in the Senate is almost endlessly debatable unless it is tabled and thereby killed.

Unobligated Balance The portion of budget authority not yet committed as payment for specific products or services. In one-year accounts, the unobligated balance expires at the end of the fiscal year for which it was made available. In multiyear accounts, it remains available for obligation for the specified number of years.

Unprinted Amendment A Senate amendment not printed in the *Congressional Record* prior to its offering. Unprinted amendments are numbered sequentially in the order of their submission through a Congress.

Upper Body A common reference to the Senate, but not used by members of the House.

Urgent Supplemental Appropriation Bill A title sometimes given to a supplemental appropriation bill for political public relations purposes. Such a title has no legal, parliamentary, or procedural significance.

U.S. Code Popular title for the *United States Code: Containing the General and Permanent Laws of the United States in Force on. . . .* It is a consolidation and partial codification of the general and permanent laws of the United States arranged by subject under fifty titles. The first six titles deal with general or political subjects, the other forty-four with subjects ranging from agriculture to war, alphabetically arranged. A supplement is published after each session of Congress, and the entire *Code* is revised every six years.

The preface to the June 1989 edition of the *Code* declares: "Because many of the general and permanent laws that are required to be incorporated in the Code are inconsistent, redundant, and obsolete, the Office of the Law Revision Counsel of the House . . . has been engaged in a continuing, comprehensive project authorized by law to revise and codify, for enactment into positive law, each title of the Code. When this project is completed all the titles of the Code will be legal evidence of the general and permanent laws and recourse to the numerous volumes of the U.S. Statutes at Large for this purpose will no longer be necessary. [As of 1989, 22 titles had been] revised, codified, and enacted into positive law and the text thereof is legal evidence of the laws therein contained. The matter contained in the other titles of the Code is prima facie evidence of the laws."

User Fee A fee charged to users of goods or services provided by the federal government. When Congress levies or authorizes such fees, it determines whether the revenues should go into the general collections of the Treasury or be available for expenditure by the agency that provides the goods or services.

V

Vacate Proceedings To nullify a chamber's previous action, such as the passage of a measure, adoption of an amendment or conference report, or an order for the yeas and nays. Requests to vacate proceedings require unanimous consent and are usually made to correct some inadvertent error in the proceedings.

Veto The president's disapproval of a legislative measure passed by Congress. He returns the measure to the house in which it originated without his signature but with a veto message stating his objections to it.

When Congress is in session, the president must veto a bill within ten days, excluding Sundays, after he has received it; otherwise it becomes law without his signature. The ten-day clock begins to run at midnight following his receipt of the bill.

Vice Chairman By House rule, the title of the ranking majority member, after the chairman, of a standing committee or subcommittee. In the Senate, the title is given only to the ranking minority member of the Indian Affairs Committee and the select committees on Ethics and Intelligence.

Views and Estimates Report A report commenting or making recommendations on budgetary matters for the upcoming fiscal year that each House and Senate committee with legislative jurisdiction must submit to the Budget committee in its house.

Voice Vote A method of voting in which members who favor a question answer "aye" in chorus, after which those opposed answer "no" in chorus, and the chair decides which position prevails.

Voting Members vote in three ways on the floor: (1) by shouting "aye" or "no" on voice votes; (2) by standing for or against on division votes; and (3) on recorded votes (including the yeas and nays), by answering "aye" or "no" when their names are called or, in the House, by recording their votes through the electronic voting system.

Voting Order on Amendments The order of precedence or priority in which pending amendments are put to a vote: First, perfecting amendments to a first degree amendment; second, perfecting amendments to a substitute amendment (but these are not permitted in the Senate); third, the substitute amendment, as amended if amended; and finally, the first degree amendment, as amended if amended.

W

Waiver A temporary setting aside of one or more rules by prohibiting points of order that might be raised to enforce them against a measure. The House uses special rules from the Rules Committee for this purpose. These rules may contain specific waivers, most frequently to protect unauthorized appropriations and legislative provisions in appropriation bills, or a blanket waiver that protects a measure or an amendment from all possible points of order.

War Powers Act of 1973 An act that requires the president "in every possible instance" to consult Congress before he commits U.S. forces to ongoing or imminent hostilities. If he commits them to a combat situation without congressional consultation, he must notify Congress within forty-eight hours. Unless Congress declares war or otherwise authorizes the operation to continue, the forces must be withdrawn within sixty or ninety days, depending on certain conditions.

The act also provides for a congressional concurrent resolution directing the president to withdraw the troops; however, in light of the Supreme Court's 1983 decision declaring legislative vetoes unconstitutional, the resolution probably would have no legal effect.

Well The sunken, level, open space between members' seats and the podium at the front of each chamber. House members usually address their chamber from their party's lectern in the well on its side of the aisle. Senators usually speak at their assigned desks.

Whip The majority or minority party member in each house who acts as assistant leader, helps plan and marshal support for party strategies, encourages party discipline, and advises his leader on how his colleagues intend to vote on the floor. In the Senate, the Republican whip's official title is assistant leader.

Whips are elected by their party caucuses. They are assisted by other party members variously called deputy whips, assistant whips, regional whips, and at-large whips.

Whip Notices Weekly communications, prepared by each party's whip in the House, advising their party's members about the following week's floor program.

Without Objection To permit an action to take place in violation of a rule, or without following the full requirements of the rules, when no member objects.

Y

Yeas and Nays A vote in which members usually respond "aye" or "no" (despite the official title of the vote) on a question when their names are called in alphabetical order. The Constitution requires the yeas and nays when a demand for it is supported by one-fifth of the members present, and it also requires an automatic yea-and-nay-vote on overriding a veto.

Yield Back the Balance of One's Time A member who controls a specific amount of time for debate is not required to use all of it, and he may give up any remaining portion of it by informing the chair that he yields back the balance of his time.

Yield the Floor To give up possession of the floor voluntarily. Senators often say, "Mr. President, I yield the floor," when they have completed their remarks. The expression is not used in the House.

Yielding A voluntary action by a member holding the floor that permits another member to speak. The member seeking permission usually asks: "Will the gentleman [senator] yield?" A member may refuse to yield or, after yielding to a colleague, may cut him off at any time.

In both houses, a member who yields for a motion, including an amendment, loses the floor. To avoid that possibility, members often announce that they are yielding for debate only. Under Senate precedents, senators may yield only for questions, but violations of those precedents are often tolerated. House members may yield for statements as well as questions.

Yielding Time When a member controls a specific amount of time for debate, another member may speak only if the controlling member yields some or all of his time for that purpose.

Because debate under a time limit is usually divided equally between proponents and opponents, the controlling member usually yields only to his supporters.

Z

Zone Whip A member responsible for whip duties concerning his or her party colleagues from specific geographical areas. Zone whips are particularly necessary in the 435-member House of Representatives, but Senate Democrats also use them.